Beyond War

Pergamon Titles of Related Interest

Boyd REGION BUILDING IN THE PACIFIC
Edmonds INTERNATIONAL ARMS PROCUREMENT
Harkavy GREAT POWER COMPETITION FOR OVERSEAS BASES
Tasca U.S.–JAPANESE ECONOMIC RELATIONS

Related Journals*

DEFENSE ANALYSIS
ECOTASS
GOVERNMENT PUBLICATIONS REVIEW
INTERNATIONAL JOURNAL OF INTERCULTURAL RELATIONS
WORLD DEVELOPMENT

*Free specimen copies available upon request.

Beyond War

Japan's Concept of
Comprehensive National Security

Robert W. Barnett

Carnegie Endowment for International Peace
Washington, D.C.

PERGAMON·BRASSEY'S
International Defense Publishers

Washington New York Oxford Toronto Sydney Paris Frankfurt

Pergamon Press Offices:

U.S.A.   Pergamon-Brassey's International Defense Publishers,
                     1340 Old Chain Bridge Road, McLean, Virginia, 22101, U.S.A

                     Pergamon Press Inc., Maxwell House, Fairview Park,
                     Elmsford, New York 10523, U.S.A.

U.K.   Pergamon Press Ltd., Headington Hill Hall,
                     Oxford OX3 0BW, England

CANADA   Pergamon Press Canada Ltd., Suite 104, 150 Consumers Road,
                     Willowdale, Ontario M2J 1P9, Canada

AUSTRALIA   Pergamon Press (Aust.) Pty. Ltd., P.O. Box 544,
                     Potts Point, NSW 2011, Australia

FRANCE   Pergamon Press SARL, 24 rue des Ecoles,
                     75240 Paris, Cedex 05, France

FEDERAL REPUBLIC Pergamon Press GmbH, Hammerweg 6,
OF GERMANY   D-6242 Kronberg-Taunus, Federal Republic of Germany

Copyright © 1984 Pergamon-Brassey's International Defense Publishers

Library of Congress Cataloging in Publication Data

Barnett, Robert W.
    Beyond war.

    Includes bibliographical references and index.
    1. Japan--National security. I. Title.
UA845.B37   1984   355'.033052   84-9249
ISBN 0-08-031617-4
ISBN 0-08-031952-1 (pbk.)

Printed in the United States of America

CONTENTS

PREFACE

I like to believe that the late John D. Rockefeller 3rd inspired the writing of *Beyond War* and its somewhat unusual format. Had he been alive, Mr. Rockefeller would have applauded the 1980 publication of the Japanese *Report on Comprehensive National Security*. His attention would have been caught immediately by the disingenuous simplicity of the first sentence of the report's official summary: "Security means protecting the people's life from various forms of threat." Being the gentle humanist that he was, he would have delighted in seeing his Japanese friends write about disparities of wealth between rich countries and overpopulated poor countries, about the world's legitimate worries over availabilities of energy and food, the need for and also the limitations on the value of weapons, and about the importance of always keeping open lines of communication even between adversaries.

When President Nixon announced to an astounded world in July 1971 that he was planning to visit Chairman Mao early in 1972, Mr. Rockefeller at once foresaw that Washington and Peking, intoxicated by this prospect, would pay little attention to how that event would affect other countries and many, if not most, of the world's ideological and strategic presuppositions. In early October 1971, Mr. Rockefeller brought to Williamsburg, Virginia 28 representatives from most of the countries of East Asia and the Pacific to talk together in a personal capacity about China's reentry into the family of nations. Japan and Southeast Asia were brilliantly represented, notably by Saburo Okita, a future foreign minister, and by Soedjatmoko, Indonesia's ambassador to the United States and a future rector of the United Nations University in Tokyo.

The great surprise of the Williamsburg Meeting was that despite an agenda that made China its centerpiece, actual discussion focused far more on Japan, its style, its vulnerabilities, and its potentials for shaping the future of its neighborhood. More remarkable still was the amazed recognition of Japanese and all other participants that once the agenda ceased to influence the question of relevance, candid talk without intention to achieve consensus produced an exhilarating sense of reality almost totally absent in other settings where Japanese and Southeast Asians had lacked the daring to speak their private minds.

In 1972 Saburo Okita and Soedjatmoko persuaded Mr. Rockefeller to convene a second "Williamsburg Meeting," which he agreed to do provided they joined him as coconveners. In later years coconveners included Alejandro Melchor of the Philippines, Thanat Kohman of Thailand, Ghazali Shafie of Malaysia, Li Choh-ming of Hongkong, Alan Renouf of Australia, Allen Lambert of Canada, Phillips Talbot and George Ball of the Asia Society in New York, and others.

Agendas differed from year to year, but mysteriously what came to be accepted as annual "Williamsburg Meetings" retained a sturdy sameness in style and even in substance. Participants attended these meetings to speak their private minds. More important, they came to listen, not to become aligned in debate but to be sobered and delighted by diverse judgments of wise and honest men of proven professional competences who had the taste and ability to leave their jargon behind. People listened, above all to what was said about the Japanese and by Japanese. Japan and China. Japan and newly industrializing countries. Japan and Vietnam. Japan and the United States. More than in any other setting participants talked frankly, even brutally, about the costs and the benefits for the region of Japan's disciplines, rigidities, and dynamism — about the threat and the protection Japan offered to its neighbors.

Beyond War takes the 1980 Japanese *Report on Comprehensive National Security* as a starting point for many private, two-way conversations during which it was my intention to listen, with only rare interposition of my own views, to what informed and responsible professionals in Washington, New York, Hawaii, Tokyo, Kyoto, and Hongkong wanted to say about the report, and, more broadly, about Japan's role in the security arrangements of the Pacific region. An intention to listen respectfully to radically contradictory assertions of fact and opinion, and a willingness to take plenty of time in doing so, yields a depth of understanding denied to anyone who demands from conversation achievement of something like agreement, accomplished in reasonably short order.

Beyond War contains my evaluation of the report, and a faithful account of what Americans, Japanese, and other Asians say about its origins, its meaning, its operational significance, and about what intimations there may be in it of Japan's future potentials for affecting other countries in Japan's neighborhood, near and far.

I could not have taken on the task of writing this little book without the active encouragement and the generous support of Thomas L. Hughes, President of the Carnegie Endowment for International Peace (and an alumnus of the Williamsburg process); former Foreign Minister Saburo Okita; Kernial Sandhu of the Institute of Southeast Asian Studies in Singapore; former Foreign Minister Kiichi Miyazawa; Chairman of Fujitsu Taiyu Kobayashi; Ambassador Richard Petree, President of the United States-Japan Foundation; and Dr. Mikio Kato of International House in Tokyo. Many others have contributed significantly to my understanding of the material I have tried to present. These include former Ambassador Nobuhiko Ushiba; Rector of the United Nations University in Tokyo Soedjatmoko; Ambassador at Large Alejandro Melchor; *Mainichi's* Bureau Chief in Washington Kasumi Kitabatake; Assistant Director of the Joint Economic Committee Richard Kaufman; Ezra Vogel at Harvard University; James Morley at Columbia University; Larry Niksch at the Congressional Research Service; Thomas Shoesmith, Deputy Assistant Secretary of State for East Asia and the Pacific; and Stephen Solarz, who presided skillfully over extended hearings on Japan held before his subcommittee of the House Foreign Relations Committee. I am, of course, particularly indebted to those who took the time to read my manuscript and offered counsel on how to elaborate upon or clarify its contents. These included Evelyn Colbert, former Deputy Assistant Secretary of State for East Asian and Pacific Affairs; Col. John Endicott of the faculty of the National Defense University; my brother, A. Doak Barnett, at Johns Hopkins University; former Assistant Secretary of State for East Asian and Pacific Affairs Marshall Green; and former Deputy Assistant Director of the Arms Control and Disarmament Agency David Linebaugh. I am, of course, particularly indebted to all those who consented to let me report on my conversations with them. They are named in the table of contents. Three of them took a continuing interest in my manuscript as a whole and offered invaluable advice, Richard J. Barnet, of the Institute for Policy Studies; Derek Davies, Editor of the *Far Eastern Economic Review*; and Gregg Rubinstein, a brilliant Japanese-speaking foreign service officer on the staff of the United States Embassy in Tokyo.

I have profited from the highly professional advice and encouragement of my friends at Pergamon.

Finally, *Beyond War* could not have been produced had I not been able to trust the fastidious scholarly conscience and the remarkable technical skills of my collaborator, Ms. Carol Goldberg. In particular, I am indebted to her for an extraordinarily complete and subtle report on a most productive Tokyo meeting — handled in the Williamsburg tradition — convened in mid-1983 by Saburo Okita and Nobuhiko Ushiba with the indispensable support of Hisahiko Okazaki, which I was unable to attend. An early version of *Beyond War* was its background document.

Robert W. Barnett
February 24, 1984

INTRODUCTION

This book is about war, in the Japanese imagination and political process. Threats to the security of Japan and the world are manifold, but for Japan the "enemy" is war. "Comprehensive security" is a Japanese term intended to describe how Japan should help to forestall, to prevent, or to limit war.

In April 1979 Prime Minister Masayoshi Ohira requested that a task force headed by Dr. Masamichi Inoki, former head of Japan's Defense Academy, prepare a study of "comprehensive national security." The task force's report was submitted to Acting Prime Minister Ito in July 1980, shortly after Prime Minister Ohira's untimely death. The report dealt with Japan's relations with the United States; Japan's position in the Pacific region and in the world; Japan's vulnerabilities with respect to energy, food, and possibilities of natural disaster; Japan's structural economic and social weaknesses at home and internationally; and inadequacies in Japan's military "denial force."

Chapter one is the English translation of the official summary of that report. To restudy it today is a reminder of the vision, realism, and idealism of its authors. Also, it raises questions.

Was the report a statement of something conceptually new, which other major countries could emulate? Or did the report merely sum up what had been the incremental and pragmatic evolution of Japan's past national security priorities and policies? Was the report announcing specific new goals, or was it merely offering rationalization for doing only what Japan had done before? Does the concept embrace elements, recognized as important but not dealt with in the report? What are these elements, often only barely alluded to?

To what extent have Japan's historic and recent experiences with war and national jeopardy affected, uniquely, its assessments of threat, its trust in dependence on allies and friends, its readiness to invest in military capability, its assessment of the gains and losses from war-fighting anywhere between anyone, and its attitudes in particular towards possession and use of nuclear weapons? Is Japan's difficulty in envisaging the fighting and winning of wars the result of its own special vulnerability or the result of seeing more clearly than others vulnerabilities actually shared by all?

If a "no-war" Japan, guided by its concept of comprehensive security, seems unable to respond effectively to Washington's charges of "free ride," will the fault be Tokyo's or Washington's? Can Tokyo improve cooperative relations with Washington, and still be faithful to the underlying psychic and philosophic no-war convictions of the Japanese people, which other countries in the region find reassuring? Or, are Washington's and Tokyo's concepts of security, global and regional, in fact incompatible? Must there be distrust, resentment, and possible collision? Or can each profit from accepting the coexistence of their two different systems, with their differing definitions of strategic goals and differing potential contributions to bringing peace to a shared world environment?

This book searches for answers to these questions in the 1980 *Report on Comprehensive National Security* itself, in the writings of many Japanese and American observers and scholars, in views expressed during private conversations I held in Washington, Honolulu, Tokyo, Hongkong, and elsewhere late in 1982 and early in 1983 with observers of and participants in the process of Pacific region-security policy formulation, and in what emerged from a small, private meeting Saburo Okita and Nobuhiko Ushiba convened in Tokyo in late March 1983, attended by Americans, Japanese, and other guests from East and Southeast Asia.

Many of these conversations took place just before, during, and after President Reagan talked with Prime Minister Nakasone in Washington, talks which brought some easing of rising hurt in Japan and anger in a United States making charges of Japan's "free ride." The talks also created both hopes and fears throughout the Pacific region about a new era in Japan's attitudes towards defense.

Communiqués, strategy pronouncements, and carefully crafted policy statements, put down in writing, are mileposts in the evolution of policy, and usually set forth expected elasticities in the scope and direction of national behavior. They merit study. Just as important, however, is listening to the way people talk, more or less off guard, about national interest and intentions, thus giving significant intimations of perhaps unadmitted but real possibilities for national commitments. That talk, in Japan, in the United States, and elsewhere, is also a part of the political process.

This book is written with the hope that members of the U.S. Congress and members of the Japanese Diet in reading about all the crosscurrents of judgment and emotion among people talking, both in Japan and the United States, will understand better that to combine the great and different potentials of Japan and of the United States in making their respective contributions to real security in the Pacific region requires patient and respectful consultation and wise and realistic adjustment, between Washington and Tokyo, of their basically different situations and capabilities.

For thirty years, a United States bearing global strategic responsibility and a Japan committed to a "no war/no collective security" national purpose, have, despite apparent cross purposes and frequent setbacks, collaborated to give East Asia's countries — from South Korea and the People's Republic of China south to Australia — the opportunity to be the growth miracle of the developing world. Japan's concept of comprehensive national security has been the backdrop for Japan's strategic calculations — and its hesitations. What does the Inoki Report say about that concept?

The first chapter contains the official summary of the task forces's 70-page report.

Beyond War

1
SUMMARY OF THE
REPORT ON COMPREHENSIVE
NATIONAL SECURITY

I. COMPREHENSIVE NATURE OF NATIONAL SECURITY POLICY

Security means protecting the people's life from various forms of threat.

Efforts required for security consist of three levels of efforts: efforts to turn the overall international environment into a favorable one; self-reliant efforts to cope with threats; and as intermediary efforts, efforts to create a favorable international environment within a limited scope while protecting security in solidarity with countries sharing the same ideals and interests.

This is true for both security in the narrow sense and economic security.

Since these three levels of efforts are mutually complementary and at the same time contradictory, it is important that balance be maintained among them.

The security question is of a comprehensive nature not only in the sense explained above but also in the sense that the fields of security interest and the means at our disposal are diverse.

II. CONDITIONS AND TASKS

a. In considering the question of Japan's security, the most fundamental change in the international situation that took place in the 1970s is the termination of clear American supremacy in both military and economic spheres.

Militarily, the military balance between the United States and the Soviet Union has changed globally and regionally as the United States has held back on strengthening its military arsenals since the mid-1960s while the Soviet Union has continued to build up its military force. As a result, U.S. military power is no longer able to provide its allies and friends with nearly full security.

As a consequence, it has become necessary for the allies and friends to strengthen their self-reliant efforts, especially in the area of conventional forces, and the credibility of the U.S. nuclear umbrella cannot be maintained in the absence of cooperation with the United States.

Economically, U.S. economic strength has declined both in absolute terms and in relative terms against the economic development achieved by Europe and Japan. As a result, it has become impossible to primarily rely upon the United States as in the past for the maintenance of the international currency system and free-trade system.

b. Another major change in the international situation has been the emergence of new powers of the South. Were the demands of the South to shift from reform to rejection of the existing system, this would constitute a major threat to the international political and economic systems.

The stable development of North-South relations is of special importance to Japan; Japan must play a major role for the developing countries' economic development and the formation of orderly North-South relations as part of its comprehensive efforts for national security.

c. The era of the "Pax Americana" upheld almost single-handedly by the United States is over, and it has given way to a new era of "peace maintained by shared responsibilities," in which all countries cooperate in the maintenance and management of the international system. It has become impossible for Japan to pursue solely its own economic interests within this system.

d. Today, Japan is enjoying unprecedented freedom and economic wealth achieved by the strenuous efforts of its people. In order to protect the political and economic systems from threat of external aggression, it is necessary for Japan to strengthen its self-reliant efforts as well as to contribute to the maintenance and strengthening of the international system.

III. ANALYSIS OF SOME SPECIFIC ISSUES

1. Relations Between Japan and the United States

a. The fundamental reason why the maintenance of close cooperative relations between Japan and the United States assumes the highest priority for Japan's comprehensive national security is that Japan shares with the United States the aspirations for the free and open international order.

b. As the relations between Japan and the United States in military, economic, cultural, and other spheres are heavily out of balance, the two countries will probably face major trials in the 1980s.

c. Given these conditions, it is necessary for Japan to build more comprehensive Japan-U.S. alliance relations as a whole and more concrete cooperation in the military field including strengthening its own defense efforts.

It is particularly important that Japan strongly support the United States when Japan feels on its own judgment that America needs to be supported.

d. With Japan now accounting for 10% of the world's total GNP, it is vital that Japan accept commensurate international responsibilities and endeavor to protect the free political, economic, and social systems.

2. Strengthening Defense Capability

a. Japan's defense policy has been based on the stance that Japan, under the Japan-U.S. security arrangements, relies upon the United States for nuclear deterrence and for the repelling of large-scale aggression, and resists small-scale and limited aggression with conventional forces by itself and prevents the easy establishment of a fait accompli. This stance to possess Japan's defense capability as a "denial force" is basically correct.

b. The problem is that the present Self-Defense Forces do not even possess the minimum necessary denial force.

As seen in the lack of a system for integrated command and control of the three sevices, the SDF has many defects in the software needed for its effective operation in the face of an emergency. In the field of combat capability, there has been neglect in making efforts to devise effective, pure self-defense, to secure survivability, and to consolidate logistic support. The lack of efforts in these areas poses problems.

Moreover, partly because the overall defense budget itself is too small, personnel and provision expenditures have come to account for much of Japan's defense spending, creating absolute weakness of arms and equipment both in quantity and in quality.

c. Equipment purchases now account for only 20% of Japan's total defense expenditure. As a result, even if this is raised to 30% in order to procure the necessary equipment, the overall increase of defense expenditure will be small. The defense expenditure will still be between 1.0% and 1.1% of GNP. The Self-Defense Forces may be able to possess substantial denial force and become meaningful by improving software aspects, studying new arms systems for purely defensive purposes, and curtailing unnecessary expenditures, while at the same time increasing defense expenditure by about 20% from the present level.

3. Relations with China and the Soviet Union

a. The reaction of the Soviet Union against the conspicuous development of Japan-China relations of late has been one that gives rise to adverse effects, and there has been a resultant deterioration in Japanese-Soviet relations. It is most undesirable for Japan's security that this be left unattended, since the Soviet Union is the only country for the time being that could pose a threat to Japan.

b. Building friendly relations with the Soviet Union is a difficult question for many countries. It is mainly due to the Soviet Union's unique philosophy of power. Expanding contact with the Soviet Union has become even more difficult since the Soviet intervention in Afghanistan. However, it will become possible and necessary to expand contacts with the Soviet Union in a few years.

c. The crux of having relations with the Soviet Union is to avoid making the Soviet Union regard Japan as either a weak or a threatening country. In other words, the question is how to harmonize the two needs, namely, to have relations with the Soviet Union in a self-confident and at the same time unhostile manner.

4. Energy Security

a. With the end of the era based upon the assumption of abundant and cheap oil, and as full-scale use of renewable energy resources will not be expected until the twenty-first century, there is a very real possibility of an energy crisis over the medium or long term.

In preparation for this, it is first necessary to work to secure global energy supply. Basically, this means promoting energy conservation, development and use of alternative energies, and the development of new energy technologies through international cooperation. In terms of practical efforts, it is important to promote cooperation among the industrialized countries and dialogue between the oil-producing and oil consuming countries in order to facilitate smooth transaction of oil, to cooperate for the oil-producing countries' industrialization, and to seek to encourage the recycling of petrodollars.

Moreover, it is necessary to make efforts to promote closer economic relations with the major oil-producing, coal-producing, and uranium-producing countries that are important to Japan and to make Japanese efforts to explore for and develop oil in the continental shelf surrounding Japan and to promote the development and use of nuclear energy and coal.

b. A short-term energy crisis is assumed to arise from such political causes as war or conflict, such physical causes as oil field accidents or tanker collisions, or such economic causes as a breakdown in negotiations for oil procurement.

In addition to international efforts, such as ensuring the effectiveness of the IEA's emergency allocation system and ensuring the safety of marine routes, Japan's own efforts, such as further enhancing its stockpiles of oil, coal, and uranium and preparing arrangements to accurately anticipate crises and to manage supply and demand appropriately in case of emergencies, are also important in dealing with this short-term situation.

5. Food Security

a. Among the conceivable threats to Japan's food security are such short-, medium-, and long-term causes as disruption of sea lanes, poor harvests in major supplying countries, deterioration of diplomatic relations with major exporting countries, and global disequilibrium in the balance between the world population and its food production.

The possibility of such crises appears remote at present and it seems that any crisis that might occur will be of limited scope and duration. However, if it should occur, the impact of a food shortage would be indeed great.

b. The argument to raise Japan's self-sufficiency in food production and the argument to abide by the principle of free trade in agricultural products both seem unrealistic. If combined with an appropriate agricultural policy, the principle of free trade can be promoted without further deterioration in Japanese agriculture.

c. This means that both international cooperation and self-reliant efforts are needed also for food security.

Among the efforts for international cooperation, it is important that we contribute to the increase of global production of foodstuffs, especially with agricultural cooperation to the developing countries in the medium- and long-term perspectives. As a short-term policy, it is necessary to establish international buffer stocks.

Concerning self-reliant efforts, in addition to maintaining a high level of potential productivity that will enable the swift increase of production in time of emergency, it is also important to study the expansion of stockpiles at all levels from consumers to the state level and the establishment of emergency distribution systems.

6. Countermeasures for Large-Scale Earthquakes — Crisis Management Systems

a. Countermeasures for large-scale earthquakes should include, first, an improved ability to predict earthquakes, and, second, the compilation both of micro-zoning maps showing the main causes of earthquake-related damage and of damage scenarios conceiving various types of disasters.

b. Based upon the above, the countermeasures must be developed in a comprehensive manner. Disaster-control considerations should be reflected in urban and regional planning, transport and traffic policies, communications policies, and all other relevant policy measures.

c. In improving the emergency management capabilities of the national and local governments for a time of emergency, it is especially important to ensure appropriate command, control, and communication mechanisms through such measures as the establishment of command and control centers with sufficient survivability and the improvement of multichannel radio communications networks.

At the same time, each household, school, and company must acquire "survival know-how" by improving independent disaster-control capabilities including the stockpiling of food, water, and medicine.

CONCLUSIONS

It is our hope that this report will serve as a catalyst for widespread and active national debate on comprehensive national security and that this will lead to productive results.

At the same time, we hope that all the ministries and agencies of the Government will bear comprehensive security considerations in mind in implementing various policy measures.

We should also like to propose the establishment of a "Comprehensive National Security Council" as a body for promoting comprehensive and integrated security policy.

We strongly hope that the proposals put forward in this report will be realized at an early date.

2
THE OUTLINE

Here is my own brief outline on Japan's concept of comprehensive national security. It summarizes some conclusions that came from my initial study of what had been written by the Inoki Task Force, and by its critics and commentators. I sent ahead this outline to be a starting point for conversation prior to most of the interviews I sought in Washington, Tokyo, Hongkong, and elsewhere. Later on in this book, I will report on the richly varied reactions provoked by this outline.

JAPAN'S STRATEGIC ENVIRONMENT

In "comprehensive national security" is shown Japan's awareness that it bears responsibilities as a superstate in a global economic system, and that it bears somewhat different responsibilities as a major power in an East Asia/Pacific neighborhood. Washington, the Association of Southeast Asian Nations (ASEAN), and Tokyo make different assessments of that shared environment.

Washington regards the Soviet Union as an enemy and expects others to share the burden of mutual security. It deplores confusion of mind over what, for Washington, is self-evident common purpose.

Partners in the ASEAN see no single outside power as clearly the common enemy. They believe that burden sharing should be intended, primarily, to sustain sound economic and social development processes. They prefer to make uneasy accommodation to, or to wait out, troublesome, even alarming, diversities and tensions that they know exist among friends — and also among adversaries — rather than to respond to outside prescription intended to clarify and gain commitment to some overriding common strategic purpose.

For Tokyo, the Soviet Union is a potential adversary, very heavily armed but otherwise vulnerable. Tokyo recognizes that burden sharing is necessary but believes that it should not be measured merely by possession of more weapons. Tokyo believes that to avoid precise articulation of common purpose can often be a source of safety.

In the Pacific region's strategic environment, differing leadership over-views, influenced of course by domestic political and economic necessity, must necessarily place restraints upon how effective mutual security policies and arrangements for East Asia and the Pacific can be worked out.

THREATS

Over time, Japan's threat perceptions have differed from Washington's, in part because the Japanese never really accepted the notion of a coherent Sino-Soviet bloc, or the reality of any significant threat from China, or the probability of any direct attack by the Soviet Union against Japan.

Japan acknowledges, of course, Washington's nuclear capabilities. It stands aside, however, far more than do countries in the North Atlantic Treaty Organization (NATO), from Washington/Moscow concerns with nuclear equivalences, deployments, disarmament, and so forth, perhaps because the Japanese very nearly exclude from their security logic any benefit from nuclear war-making under any circumstances. Tokyo was given a jolt by the prospect of added SS-20 redeployments east of the Urals.

Among dangers that most alarm Tokyo are fear of losing access to over-seas sources of food and energy (see Appendix I), fear that Washington may be indifferent to Japan's need for vital imports and its need for access to the American and other markets, fear of loss of acceptability as an active partner in the economic growth dynamic of Southeast Asia, fear of a break-down of the international system, and fear of surges of great disorder anywhere.

There is, in addition, fear of Soviet strategic miscalculation "due to the Soviet Union's unique philosophy of power," symbolized by Russia's "irra-tional" creation of military installations on the Northern Islands, its han-dling of Japanese fishing rights, and its behavior in Kampuchea and Afghanistan, with respect to Poland, and so forth. Japan remembers a major war won against Czarist Russia and seriously troubled relations with Moscow periodically throughout this century. Tokyo is well informed about Russia's current build-up of naval, air, and missile capability in East Asia but is less inclined than Washington to attribute to Moscow any unremitting or irrever-sibly sinister intention.

THE CONCEPT

The July 1980 *Report on Comprehensive National Security* deals descrip-tively and prescriptively with the concept which should underlie Japan's secu-rity planning.

The concept antedated by many years the formulation of the term "com-prehensive" to describe it. The concept evolved within the framework of

Article 9 of the Constitution;[1] the first and second United States-Japan security treaties of 1952 and 1960; creation of the Self-Defense Forces in 1954; resumption of "normal" relations with the U.S.S.R. in 1956; enunciation of the three nuclear principles – no production, possession, or introduction of weapons; and normalization of relations with the People's Republic of China in 1972. With growth of Japan's formidable economic powers (see Appendices II and III), there was also recognition of Japan's responsibility to enter into bilateral aid commitments; to make large contributions to the International Monetary Fund, the World Bank, and other international financial institutions; to strengthen and stabilize the world economy by other appropriate measures; and to make constructive diplomatic responses to crisis situations abroad. All of this preceded publication of the report.

In considering the actual national commitments called for by the concept of comprehensive national security, Japan has always confronted the task of reconciling competitive/conflicting strategic interests. Japan has wanted to keep faith with Article 9 of its Constitution. Japan has wanted to avoid behavior likely to excite alarm elsewhere in East Asia, notably in Korea, China, and the ASEAN area. Japan has wanted to contribute to effective functioning of a worldwide, nondiscriminatory, competitive economic system through aid, trade liberalization, and collaboration in making structural adjustments in the system. Japan has felt an acute need to anticipate emergencies arising from interruption of access to food and energy (see Appendix I), or emergencies caused by national disasters at home. Japan has understood, of course, both the benefits and the obligations flowing from the United States-Japan security treaties. It has understood the necessity of anticipating tactical requirements of conventional military engagement with the Soviet Union. And, with increasing bewilderment and frustration, Japan has tried, in various ways, to forestall growth in the virulence of "free ride" charges made against Japan in the United States and elsewhere.

The concept of comprehensive security required reconciliation of these interests and purposes. As a practical matter, that reconciliation takes place every year during a bureaucratic and legislative budget process in which Japan's central concern has always been the competitive effectiveness – even survival – of Japan's dynamic but vulnerable economy. The budget process has defined and still defines Japan's national priorities. "Comprehensive national security" does not prescribe exactly what the priorities should be, but the concept helps to interpret what strategic meaning should be attributed to Japan's exacting budget process. Prime Minister Nakasone, despite a style of leadership different from his predecessors, accepts, as did they, the disciplines of that process: in a sense that process is Japan's sovereign voice.

ECONOMIC INTERDEPENDENCE:
PRECONDITION FOR SECURITY

Administration of a stable, growth-oriented, and reliably outward-looking/
interdependent economic system is the bedrock of Japan's own security and
by far Japan's greatest contribution to the security of other countries in the
East Asian region. This can be asserted with great confidence because Japan,
as a buyer and seller of goods, capital, technology, and management, has
been the most steady external contributor to economic growth throughout
the entire East Asian neighborhood; that growth has been a precondition
for popular acceptance of the legitimacy of governments everywhere.

Whereas Japan's growth, low rate of inflation, low interest rates, high
rate of savings, low rate of unemployment, and brilliant achievements in
management and technology have presented testing/pace-setting challenges
to the United States and other highly industrialized countries, for East Asia,
the Japanese "locomotive," even under strain, has been seen as an anchor
of security, and as a source of hope for continued growth. This was noticed
particularly in the late 1970s and early 1980s when uncertainties about United
States growth, interest rates, inflation, unemployment, and protectionist
inclinations carried threatening implications for other East Asian countries
(see Appendix II). Both the *Asian Wall Street Journal's* and the *Far Eastern
Economic Review's* data on the performance and outlook of the East Asian
economies for 1982-1983 showed how profoundly, country by country, in-
stability in the United States and stability in Japan affected the day-to-day
security calculations of these countries.[2]

All of Japan's East Asian trading partners, respecting Japan's achievement, also desire, perhaps even more than countries in the Organization for
Economic Cooperation and Development (OECD), much easier access to
Japan's "protected" markets. They also believe that Japan should extend more
and easier aid along all the lines referred to in the *Report on Comprehensive
National Security*. For 1980, aggregate official development assistance (ODA)
and defense expenditures as percentage of gross national product amounted
to: U.S., 5.8%; U.K., 5.4%; France, 4.6%; West Germany 3.6%; Australia, 3.3%; Japan, 1.3%.[3] A critical difficulty, in judging fairly the real
meaning of such comparisons which place Japan in a bad light, both as trading partner and as contributor to burden sharing, is the over-strong dollar
and the weak yen, an exchange rate disparity that Japan deplores, and for
which Japan is not necessarily to blame (see Appendix IV).

KNOWLEDGE IS POWER

An underlying assumption in Japanese thinking about national interest
and effectiveness is that the possession of voluminous, accurate, and usable
information is a paramount strategic asset. Japan's educational system, the

sophistication of its knowledgeable business community, Japan's intense attention to potentials of technology and to scrupulous quality control, and Japan's avid interest in cultural and technological borrowings worldwide — starting with China over a thousand years ago — confirm commitment to the idea that knowledge is power.

Japan now recognizes its interdependences and its responsibility to assist in sustaining their mutual value, but a premise underlying Japan's willingness to contribute its economic, scientific, technological, and human resources to other countries is that it should have specific knowledge about their purposes and the likely consequences of their use: only then can Japan know how to help. "Wholesale" aid is not in Japan's character: a requirement for knowledge about probable results, in part, explains Japan's preference for "tied aid" and accounts for its high quality.

Japan is unsuccessful in taking credit for its prudent "zero error" approaches to national difficulty/opportunity. Japan does very poorly in keeping its books — for readers in Japan and abroad — so as to quantify comprehensively its ODA, its creation of food and energy stocks, its technological transfers, and its cultural exchange contributions to "comprehensive security." For example, hardly noticed by anyone, even in Japan, is Japan's recently substantial "comprehensive security" aid to Egypt, Turkey, Pakistan, and Thailand. Japan, moreover, is almost totally inarticulate in explaining to its own people or to others what knowledge it must have to effectively restructure, and if necessary to increase its national defense capabilities. Media and public reaction to Prime Minister Nakasone's January visit to Washington focused on and generated excitement over a few symbolically hawkish remarks and gestures rather than drawing attention to the fundamental economic, institutional, military, and philosophical factors in the predicament being faced, together, by Washington and Tokyo.

KNOWLEDGE AS DETERRENCE

Japan faces a dilemma: to present a low military profile invites charges of "free ride" from Americans — and some Europeans — but to declare intent to invest more heavily in weapons provokes for all others, friends and adversaries, fears of Japanese remilitarization and/or destabilizing superpower aspiration. Japan must, therefore, devise such specific military undertakings as can demonstrate the reality of increased military effectiveness without violating the "only for defense" interpretation of Japan's no-war Constitution, which all of Japan's neighbors want Japan to respect. A chapter of the *Report on Comprehensive National Security,* harshly criticizes Japanese misuse and mismanagement of its defense appropriations. In it there is reference, unfortunately only suggestive, to how, at moderate cost, there might be high military return from Japanese research and development (R and D), and from use of Japan's great electronic and computer skills in the military sector without, thereby, inviting the charge of beginning to show offensive capability.[4]

Prime Minister Suzuki's promise to undertake defense out 1000 nautical miles alarmed several of Japan's neighbors and prompted back-tracking explanations to the Japanese Diet. Washington, of course, applauded Suzuki's commitments to expand Japan's military responsibilities. If, however, those commitments – now reconfirmed by Prime Minister Nakasone – continue to provoke excessive and possibly needless, anxieties within Japan and elsewhere, then Washington should explore further with Japan clarification of how Japan could gain better combat effectiveness within an unassailably "defense only" framework.

Since knowledge is power, Japan should gather information about all the strategic/tactical possibilities in Northeast Asia, using Japanese facilities. With its own justification and motive, Japan could then invest, without waste, in that precise panoply of Japanese naval, air, and ground forces needed to forestall intimidation, and to make possible, if ever attacked, smart and punishing response. Ground-based command of Tsushima, Tsugaru, and Soya, and sea approaches to these straits, give Japan great geographic war-deterring assets. But the crucial precondition for a wisely adequate Japanese investment in some limited but effective war-fighting capability – a genuine denial force – is, I believe, a Japanese capacity to make its own evaluation of threat – not in a global but in its own regional environment.

For Japan to *advertise* a very conspicuous reliance on a high-cost airborne warning and control system (AWACS)[5] – located, for example, in Hokkaido and in Kyushu – might be understood as a shorthand way of describing to all of Japan's neighbors Japan's intention to acquire an elaborately comprehensive, high-technology capability: radar, electronic, acoustic, photographic, and cryptographic. Use of AWACS would be coordinated by Army, Navy, and Air Self Defense Forces for gathering exhaustive and swiftly retrievable military information strictly for defensive purpose. Japanese and American negotiators, already, are moving towards something like such a system, upgrading Basic Air Defense Ground Environment (BADGE), without so far using "AWACS" as the term to characterize its great capability, and its "defense only" usefulness. Washington should, and would, encourage Tokyo to go forward towards developing such a threat-analysis capability as efficiently as possible: if this capability became, over time, as good as that of the United States, all would be gainers. Knowledge is the cure for paranoia.

Tokyo's commitment to such a "defense only" undertaking might ease gaining acquiescence from the Japanese Diet and public for higher levels of defense spending. Procurement from the United States of high-cost equipment should mute charges of "free ride" in Washington. Collaboration with Washington could yield critically valuable benefits, technologically and in eventual tactical potentials for supporting the U.S. presence in the region, even though the nature of that implicit support capability would not need to be advertised. No country in Southeast Asia would object to Japanese spending for such a "defense only" undertaking.

Nakasone's 1970 Defense White Paper was the first Japanese proclamation dealing explicitly with the problem of security. In it he challenged the proposition that great economic power necessitated possession of great military power: and, to him have been attributed the two concepts of having "long ears" and being a "porcupine." AWACS should be talked about as serving those purposes only.

Japan needs to talk more openly about contributions it can make to mutual security, nonmilitary and even paramilitary. In a nuclear strategic environment "security" is ambiguous, except in one regard: there is improved security in knowledge. Having that in mind, Japan might, by way of illustration, help ASEAN countries, if requested, in furnishing Japanese technological and financial support for a Southeast Asian *nonmilitary* "Coast Guard," responsible for performing from the South China Sea to the Indian Ocean all the functions of the kind now carried on by the United States Coast Guard for the United States or Japan's Maritime Safety Agency for Japan. Its facilities, at sea, in the air, at shore stations, and on satellites, would gather information freely available to everyone on what was happening "down there." Such an enterprise would be entirely consistent with strategic concepts underlying ASEAN's Zone of Peace, Freedom and Neutrality, and with Article 9 of the Japanese Constitution: it would increase safety at sea and largely reduce doubts as to what, actually, might be the precise motive of air and sea activity in the region.[6]

NUCLEAR POWER

By the 1990s, Japan will have exceeded by at least two times what all the rest of East Asia will have invested in nuclear generating power and in the technology of reprocessing and disposing of nuclear waste. Japan appears to be irreversibly committed to commercial use of breeder reactors. Neighboring Korea, Taiwan, and several ASEAN countries will be increasingly attentive to Japan's success in assuring itself in this way the energy resources needed for survival of its economic system. Now content to rely upon the United States and France, they may soon want to explore ways to profit from what may be expected to be Japanese preeminence in assuring safety in the use of nuclear energy for economic purpose. Growing nuclear power-generating capacity in East Asia will bring, of course, a theoretical capability to fabricate nuclear explosives in a matter of months. Tokyo is in a strong position to reinforce nuclear non-proliferation commitments throughout all of East Asia because its own theoretical capacity to produce nuclear explosives is clear, because of Japan's intimate economic interdependence with nearby South Korea and Taiwan — potentially volatile irredentist countries — and because Japan's experience with the consequences of actual nuclear war gives psychically intense popular support to its outspoken official commitments to the purposes of the Non-Proliferation Treaty.

Japan's comprehensive security doctrine suggests that Japan should use all of its rich intellectual, diplomatic, political, economic, and scientific resources to forestall the calamity of war. So far, Japan has stood a little back from recommending/supporting various worldwide arms control proposals or from taking a public stand on such difficult issues as "no first use" of nuclear weapons. However, in many nonspecific ways, Japan is committed to moving in nonnuclear, peace-promoting, war-preventing directions.

Not to be entirely excluded from possibilities, however, is a tragic turn of events that could cause Japanese leadership to move in an opposite direction. Such events might include a breakdown of confidence in the effectiveness of the American system, bewilderment and dismay over "irrational" vertical proliferation of nuclear weapons in the U.S.–Soviet arms race, horizontal proliferation of nuclear weapons with risk of their use by fanatic or adventuristic regimes, or insulting and abusive treatment of Japan by other countries leading the Japanese people to feel that such condescension revealed scorn for a "powerless" Japan.

3
PACIFIC REGION OVERVIEWS

Throughout conversations about comprehensive security with non-Americans in Washington I was constantly reminded that the United States, Japan, and Southeast Asian countries clearly have different conceptions of what operating premises should guide responses to the strategic realities of the East Asian and Pacific regions. I tried to sort out, before moving forward with my interviews, what I believed to be differences in the U.S., Japanese, and Southeast Asian overviews — their perceptions of reality.

THE UNITED STATES

The Department of State's 1982 overview of East Asia and the Pacific is familiar to almost anyone who has read speeches by secretaries and assistant secretaries over recent years. Observers of the region can recite from memory most of its elements.

The United States, with great consistency, has opposed domination of the region by any single power, has sought access to all parts of the region, and has been committed to constructive involvement in the political, economic, and cultural life of the diverse societies throughout the region.

The United States takes satisfaction from the economic, political, and security relations that have been maturing between the United States and Japan, and recognizes that a strong and dynamic Japan is the locomotive carrying along with it the remarkable growth processes of many neighboring countries. It recognizes that among great economic powers strains are inevitable: they can be solved with patience and readiness to deal with them jointly. The United States/Japan Alliance is a linchpin in security arrangements for the region.

The United States takes satisfaction, considering the differing traditions and systems of the two countries, in what has been successful progression towards normalization of diplomatic relations with the People's Republic of China, a process that carries great political, economic, cultural, and security implications for the region. Taiwan presents intractable difficulty.

The global implications of a build-up of Soviet military capabilities in Eastern Siberia, at sea, and in present and potential base facilities within the region seriously affect a previous U.S. position of unmistakable military superiority throughout the region.

Washington must be alert to the possibility of turmoil arising from transfers of power from present national leadership into new hands, notably in the Philippines and in Indonesia, but also, possibly, in the two Koreas, Taiwan, the People's Republic of China, and even Singapore.

Unexpected convulsions within countries could erupt in several places that would affect the entire region. A war could break out in Korea, possibly as a result of North Korean exploitation of a breakdown of effective leadership or efficient functioning of the economy in South Korea: this is an event of low probability. Good relations between the United States and Japan could be undermined by sustained, provocative, and vengeful protectionism on the U.S. side, or by feelings of mutual betrayal or impotence, by both sides towards the other, in working towards satisfactory security arrangements: this prospect is of very low probability. If a failure in China's ambitious and exacting modernization strategies brought about the humiliation and rejection of Deng Xiaoping and his surrogates, China, in desperation, might commence unpredictable and disturbing activity: there are no signs that this is probable.

In the coming period, the United States will be trying to preserve a region-wide (also a worldwide) open and competitive trading system, trying to invite the cooperation of other countries in sharing the military burden of security, and trying to contribute, as practical, to economic development processes within and among all the countries of the region except North Korea and Vietnam.

Despite its worries, Washington is optimistic about the prospect for achieving its near future goals. Looking beyond the 1980s, however, there will necessarily be uncertainties about successes in solving, nationally and regionally, such structural problems as population growth, adequate food production, meeting energy requirements, and coping with pathological urbanization.

Everything considered, Washington is satisfied with its definition of foreign policy goals and with its success in pursuing them in the East Asian/ Pacific region. Officers responsible for relations with the East Asian Pacific region like to invite comparison of their achievements with the achievements of those responsible for U.S. relations with Western Europe, Africa, Latin America, and South Asia, not to mention with the Soviet Union.

Several operating premises seem to underlie the American overview:

• The Soviet Union is our common enemy.

• Others should help to cover costs of the needed arms build-up and to ease the overloading of U.S. economic capabilities resulting from responding to the Soviet threat; this is burden sharing.

- And, the United States deplores any confusion of mind over what is regarded as a self-evident common purpose; this is the basis for charges of "free ride."

JAPAN

Tokyo has another overview.

Tokyo, as Prime Minister Nakasone told President Reagan, regards its place in the world community as inextricably linked to understandings with the United States; to the U.S.-Japan Security Treaty; to common commitment with Washington to preservation of a worldwide competitive, non-discriminatory economic system; and to sharing with Washington proper responsibility for helping to preserve peace and improve the general welfare of peoples in the region. Tokyo has understood, however, that the era of Pax Americana is over, and that reduction of real U.S. military and economic predominance creates new problems but also, perhaps, new opportunities — some separate, and some shared — for Japan and other countries in the region.

Tokyo welcomes normalization of its relations with Peking, wants to improve those relations, and tries to respect Chinese sensitivities on issues like Taiwan. Japan may, sometimes, be skeptical about how deeply it should be involved in China's modernization strategies: Japan wishes them well, but not too well, perhaps. At some future time, China could become a formidable competitor.

Southeast Asia and Oceania figure prominently in Tokyo's relations within the region. Australia's trade with Japan is significantly larger than with the United States. Indonesia's is almost three times larger. Malaysia's and Thailand's are larger. Trade with Japan and with the United States is about the same for the Philippines and Singapore.[7] These trade ties are a startling achievement for a country whose population and GNP are about half those of the United States.

Tokyo has various reasons for promoting this trend: need for raw materials, desire to expunge ugly memories of the past, and a need to assure a secure neighborhood for sea-lanes through which vital energy imports from the Middle East must come (see Appendix I).

Japan is sensitive to explosive possibilities in the divided countries of the region, China, Korea, and Vietnam. But Tokyo has followed the practice of separating politics from economics, and trades with all factions within these areas. Fourteen percent of North Korea's trade is with Japan; 21% of South Korea's; 21% of Laos'; 25% of China's; and 19% of Taiwan's.[8]

The Soviet Union poses the only military threat to Japan, and Tokyo has observed that relations with Moscow deteriorate as relations with Peking improve. Soviet behavior in the Northern Islands and in fishing controversies —

not to mention in places like Afghanistan, Kampuchea, and Poland — offends
Japan. However, Tokyo does not refer to the Soviet Union as an enemy,
but only as an adversary having strengths, but also serious vulnerabilities.

Japan knows that despite its three nuclear principles and the no-war Article 9 of its Constitution, Japan will never be a pacifist state. Prime Minister
Nakasone's readiness to allow public discussion of these commitments does
not foreshadow likely change of Japan's basic strategic intentions. Spending
about 1% of its GNP on its military establishment, the $12 billion Japan
devotes to its annual defense budget is the sixth largest defense expenditure
among the free-world nations. Japan deploys twice as many destroyers in
the region as does the Seventh Fleet and more tactical aircraft than are
deployed by the United States in Japan, the Republic of Korea, and the Philippines together. The United States military services are gratefully aware of
all this, and welcome Japan's readiness to accept responsibility for control
of sea-lanes out to a distance of 1000 nautical miles, south from Osaka and
southeast from Tokyo. However, largely absent from Japanese literature is
discussion of scenarios for actual military engagement, except occasionally,
as when Prime Minister Nakasone referred to the straits through which Soviet
warships must pass in returning to or leaving bases in the Sea of Japan.

Conspicuously, Japan's overview of the region is introspective, shaped
by obsessive awareness of its economic vulnerabilities and influenced by profound distrust of military remedies anywhere, for anyone. In the Japanese
imagination, the supreme threat is war itself.

Several operating premises seem to underlie the Japanese overview:

• The Soviet Union is an enemy for the United States, but for Japan, Russia
  is a vulnerable adversary with which continuing talk is essential.

• The United States wants burden sharing to cope effectively with a global
  enemy, but for Japan it is not obvious that Washington should assign to
  Japan and others even the specific regional burdens to be borne.

For the United States, lack of articulated common purpose among friends
is deplorable, but for Japan in diversities of national intention and behavior
among neighbors, both friends and adversaries, there is as often safety as
danger (e.g., between China and the Soviet Union, between the Soviet Union
and Vietnam, between Bangkok and Jakarta, and even between the United
States and Japan). There should be low visibility maneuver, not confrontation, both with friends and with adversaries.

SOUTHEAST ASIA

No single overview can be attributed to Southeast Asia. There are,
however, common elements in what is seen by observers in that region. Even

this represents a dramatic transformation of the configuration and dynamic of societies in that region since World War II. In great contrast to the situation before World War II, no Southeast Asian country depends today upon any power external to the region for sustaining national authority.

There are common elements in the overviews of Southeast Asian countries. Pax Americana persists in the imaginations of leaders and people throughout Southeast Asia, but its luster has been blemished by Washington's unseemly retreat from Saigon, alarming implications of the incredible decline of American economic strength and competitiveness, concern over Washington's "overcommitment" to Peking and its "exaggeration" of Soviet power, and recurrent alarm at possible consequences of continuing tension between Washington and Tokyo.

Japan is now the power in the Pacific region whose example, resources, and behavior make the greatest and steadiest day-to-day contribution in the growth processes of all Southeast Asian countries. Until very recently Japan was seen as lacking deployable military capability, and not having much military capability at all. Almost unanimously, Southeast Asians oppose significant "remilitarization" of Japan.

Southeast Asian countries are obsessed by a vision of the power that they suppose is inherent in the size and population of the Chinese landmass. This seeming paranoia is given credibility by the extraordinary economic, intellectual, and organizational achievements of Chinese minorities within their own countries and by knowledge of China's past involvement, both open and clandestine, in local insurgency movements. Another dimension of paranoia arises from fear that "Chinese" achievement in Taiwan, Hongkong, and Singapore will be matched, one day, on the Chinese mainland.

Southeast Asia views the Soviet Union through bifocals. For distance vision they use glass ground in Washington, and accept Washington's assessment of global strategic balances, nuclear and otherwise. Looking through glass ground locally Southeast Asians see substantial increase in Soviet naval activity, Moscow's at least $3-4 million daily subsidy to Hanoi, and Moscow's access, with Hanoi's acquiescence, to Cam Ranh Bay and Danang. However, they see little that shows really effective Russian Communist links, subversive, cultural, or economic, elsewhere in their region. Southeast Asia's evaluation of the Soviet role in the region is a softer version of Japan's — an enemy of their system but a vulnerable military adversary. For some Southeast Asians, Moscow is a possibly useful counterweight to Peking.

ASEAN's chiefs of state do not now look outside for solution of problems inside, nor do they want it. Their goal is the ultimate establishment of a Zone of Peace, Freedom, and Neutrality, including Vietnam, from which strategic involvement by the Soviet Union, China, Japan, and the United States would be removed. They believe that Vietnam, without external aid, could be managed.

Southeast Asian operating premises seem to be:

- No outside power is clearly the only enemy.

- The principal objective of burden sharing should be to enlist assistance from affluent countries to sustain economic and social development.

- Acceptable coexistence is more likely to be gained by accommodation to intractable and perhaps long-term diversities than by seeking precise definition of comprehensive common purpose.

4
CONVERSATIONS IN WASHINGTON WITH SOME JAPANESE

Washington abounded with "authorities" ready to advance views on some one or another aspect of Japan's attitude towards Pacific region security arrangements. Many of these specialists had heard of the term "comprehensive security." However, few had read the Inoki Report. Fewer had had the time or even much inclination to place reconciliation of Tokyo's and Washington's differences within Tokyo's "comprehensive" framework. I made it my intention to elicit views from these people on Japan's concept of comprehensive security by inviting them to receive my outline and to comment on it as systematically as they desired. Almost invariably, talk would focus rather narrowly on Japan's "free ride," Japan's "quixotic" perceptions of threat, the optimum military role to be played by Japan, and, quite often, on the United States' own responsibility for being the cause of many persistent Tokyo-Washington tensions. In rare cases, there was detailed talk about the Inoki Report.

Unstructured conversation is a part of the policy process and, if loosely guided, can reveal crosscurrents and contradictions in policy intentions.

During my interviews I let my outline represent my views. My role was to listen. Sometimes I made notes. Sometimes, I recorded recollection only subsequently. None of my conversations was taped. What follows here is not a verbatim record of what others actually said. I could record only what I understood them to be saying: there is a great difference. Responsibility for what came out of talk is mine, not the speakers'.

As shown in the table of contents, I have selected 54 conversations — out of more than 150 — for inclusion in this book. There is a logical reason for my having grouped them as I have. And before moving from one grouping of interviews to the next I will explain what special significance I attached to each, individually and collectively. In the interviews, themselves, I will let my respondents speak for themselves; I will not try to interpret or pass judgment on what they say. But I will say why what they say interests me.

In my first grouping are six Japanese whom I met in Washington. All had a professional responsibility for being well acquainted with trends in Japan, to be familiar with trends in the United States, and to speak knowledgeably about national security matters, Japanese and American. Abe, Washington Bureau Chief of *Sankei,* was frank to confess that his paper has a recognized right-wing promilitary bias: he was troubled by the propensity of Japanese to swing to great extremes, and quite quickly. Kitabatake, Washington Bureau Chief of *Mainichi,* explained that his paper stands in the political spectrum about where the *Washington Post* stands in the American spectrum: he reflected on why Japanese could analyze the threat of the Soviet Union differently than the United States. Saito, at the International Monetary Fund, dwelt on how it could be possible to know, with great certainty, that Japan's economy was good for the region, and still be unable to offer quantitative proof. Nishihara, of the Japanese Defense Academy, dealt with most of the points contained in the outline, often with a confidence that could only be based upon knowledge shared by Japanese defense intellectuals. Ogoshi, of Japan's Defense Agency, cast light on Japan's motivations in procuring needed equipment from American producers. Ambassador Okawara made succinct comment on the outline, noting, in particular, that everyone's security depended on avoiding a serious and prolonged American depression; and, probably inescapably, differences in Washington's global and Tokyo's regional perspectives on weapons requirements would create difficulties.

Americans in Washington and Japanese in Tokyo would allude to all of these matters, but perhaps with less detachment and less confidence in the importance of the issues that concerned these sophisticated Japanese "expatriates."

YASUNORI ABE, *SANKEI*
(July 21, 1982)

Yasunori Abe, Chief of the Washington bureau of *Sankei,* in a talk with me about "comprehensive security" before his expected return to Tokyo, reminded me that *Sankei* was unmistakably more conservative than *Mainichi, Asahi,* and *Yomiuri* on foreign policy issues. Even so, by American standards, Japanese right-wingers on defense issues were quite moderate, he said.

Abe dwelt on what he believed was a special quality in the Japanese character, a propensity for sudden swings of emotional overcommitment. Japanese, as a group, on short notice, could go to great extremes. Abe believed that controversy in Japan on defense issues, and stubborn insistence on certain principles of self-denial, arose from a Japanese awareness that it must learn from past experience and create structures that forestall release of ill-considered Japanese passions.

Japan had developed a broad consensus in support of alliance with the United States and moderately but steadily increased investment in Japan's Self Defense Forces. But it was also true, he said, that there was a growing majority in business, in the bureaucracy, and in the Diet—and in some elements of the media—that had begun to believe that humiliating exposure to threats and bullying tactics by the United States and Western Europe could be attributed to Japan's possession of only negligible military capability.

Abe did not forecast an early surge of Japanese national intention to become a major military power. However, he did warn that Japan's present commitments to pacifism and only a limited investment in its military establishment could be replaced by doing something quite different, which would not primarily be justified by military threats presented by China or by the Soviet Union. Abe pointed out the possibility that too much pressure on Japan by the United States on trade matters could backfire, and when reassessment of relations with the United States came it might be quite sudden and quite extreme.

I told Abe that, quite contrary to what he was suggesting, the Japanese seemed to be extraordinarily unaffected by emotional factors in their systematic and ruthlessly realistic annual evaluation of national requirements. One of the effects of post-Occupation constitutional democracy had been to diminish greatly the possibility of extremism: such extremism would have to survive exposure to exhaustive debate in the annual budget process. Abe admitted that he had not thought about the Japanese system in those terms, and was not, himself, convinced that even with this democratic system the risks of extremism were removed. He said emotional swings were inherent in Japanese society. Moreover, the temperature inside Japan regarding the United States was going up slowly, although it was still far short of an explosive point.

In Abe's opinion, large-scale remilitarization of Japan could easily include a decision to produce a sophisticated nuclear weapons capability. Abe admitted that support of that view on paper might not be easy to find. Nuclear weaponry was a taboo subject. If there was Japanese advocacy of production, possession, or use in certain quarters it was likely to be quiet, oblique, and suggestive.

YASUHIRO OGOSHI, JAPAN DEFENSE AGENCY
(August 26, 1982)

Yasuhiro Ogoshi, visiting the United States under the auspices of the Meridian House Visitor Program Service, was soon to become director of the Central Procurement Office of the Japanese Defense Agency. While in Washington, Ogoshi had visited the Department of State, the Department of Defense, the National Security Council, the Joint Chiefs of Staff, and the Heritage Foundation.

Ogoshi reviewed Japan's next five-year program with its intention to procure fighter aircraft, surveillance aircraft, radar, mine sweeping and laying equipment, destroyers, tanks, command-control-communications, ammunition and spare parts stockpiles, and so forth.

I told Ogoshi that I kept looking for a Japanese explanation of how procurement was designed to help to refute the charge of "free ride," without increasing anxieties of Japan's neighbors. I referred, in that connection, to the logic of my "AWACS concept." Ogoshi responded that the currently intended investment in surveillance and command-control-communications apparatus, modernization of radar, and the purchase of eight E-2Cs was quite in line with my thinking about the symbolic value of "AWACS." The rather large orders of F-15s would have a balance-of-payments impact favorable to Washington. Ogoshi also pointed out that the United States had a rather good surveillance capability in the region, and might dislike Japanese competition. He said that American authorities were pressuring Japan to spend more for things Washington wants to sell: fighters, destroyers, antisubmarine vessels, and stockpiles of ammunition and spare parts.

KASUMI KITABATAKE, *MAINICHI*
(September 10, 1982)

Kasumi Kitabatake, Washington bureau chief of *Mainichi,* offered views on Japan's concept of threat. Japan clearly understood the Soviet threat. However, because Japan had ignored, for so long, problems of national defense, it had been obliged, until recently, to acquiesce with very little questioning to Washington's facts and analysis of the Soviet threat. Independent Japanese analysis was superficial and vague. In fact, Japan failed to sort out various elements in the Russian threat. Soviet weapons were obviously one element. But there were many other elements — population, its composition, and its location. There was also the factor of economic capability. Japanese could agree that Russian weapons were a danger and still accord greater importance to other considerations in making strategic calculations about the Soviet Union. It was natural — even inevitable — that Japanese would always have in mind the enormous disparities in size of the two countries, their proximity to each other, and an increasing need to explore modes of coexistence. Canada and Mexico made such calculations, as neighbors of the United States. Finland accommodated, in its way, to the Soviet Union. Japan, in its own way, must cope with that necessity.

MASASHI NISHIHARA, DEFENSE ACADEMY
(November 26, 1982)

Masashi Nishihara, as a professor at Japan's National Defense Academy, and as a Rockefeller Foundation Fellow in New York, had written highly respected essays on Japan's security problems for the *New York Times,* the *Washington Quarterly* of Georgetown University, and other journals. He made comment on my outline quite systematically.

Japan's budgetary process, he reminded me, was influenced by Japanese interparty politics. How the opposition parties reacted to the government's defense efforts or security measures played an important role in what government policy could, as a practical matter, be.

It was true, Nishihara said, that the Japanese concept of comprehensive security antedated by many years invention of the term itself, notably in an international strategic environment over which loomed the oil shocks and a decline of U.S. oil majors' control over the oil supply from the Middle East.

Some opposition elements in Japan used to argue that the Liberal Democratic Party (LDP) was trying to camouflage increasing defense costs within the comprehensive security concept. Actually, the government was using the concept to give a basis for fending off American "free ride" criticism. Knowing this, other critics charged that the concept could not fend off the "free ride" charges for very long, because "comprehensive security" budget allocations, if realistically calculated, would have to be raised annually by 10%, or even more, which the government had no intention of doing.

Other skeptics said that talk about "comprehensive security" induced complacency about the nation's security. Economic aid to Thailand could not help Japan to cope with the growing Soviet military deployment in the Northwest Pacific, or such a possibility as war in Korea. With the growing deployment of Soviet nuclear forces in Soviet Asia and the Western Pacific, Nishihara wondered whether Japan could afford to stick to its three nuclear principles.

Japan's administration of its economic system, Nishihara observed, had some shortcomings. Energetic export promotion caused resentment against Japanese business among Asians (as well as, of course, among some Americans).

As to "knowledge is power," the "voluminous, accurate, and immediately retrievable information" to which I had referred was very important for Japan, but Japanese governments, strangely, had not emphasized this point. Nakasone himself had talked about the need for Japan to become "a rabbit having long ears," meaning Japan needed to possess extensive foreign military, political, and economic intelligence.

The "AWACS concept," as an example of "knowledge as deterrence," might present some difficulties:

• Would neighboring nations regard AWACS as "defensive"?

• If AWACS were to fly within limited boundaries, what should such delineation be?

- The United States liked to have all basic available military intelligence under its own control. Washington might not like to let Japan have the AWACS capability.

- Could investment in AWACS undermine the priority that should be given to the defense of the home islands and the sea-space out 1000 nautical miles?

- If AWACS planes ever had to make emergency landings in Asia, such landings would be criticized as "forces going abroad."

Japan might do better by helping to finance U.S. AWACS operations out of Clark Airfield in the Philippines, and Southeast Asian nations might prefer to see the U.S. military presence enhanced rather than to see a new Japanese "military" presence introduced.

The idea of a Japan-supported Southeast Asian nonmilitary Coast Guard was more interesting and might be more feasible politically.

Nishihara commented that to advocate that all nations should condemn morally the first use of nuclear weapons sounded nice. However, Japan was in a dilemma. To advocate "no first use" would deny, at least partly, the U.S. nuclear umbrella. It could cause Washington to press Tokyo to increase its own conventional arms build-up. The Japanese government could not really take a clear stand in favor of "no first use."

KUNIO SAITO, INTERNATIONAL MONETARY FUND
(December 22, 1982)

Kunio Saito, assistant director in the Asian Division of the International Monetary Fund (IMF), knew that I sought from him statistical reinforcement for some of the themes of my outline.

Saito agreed with the proposition in the outline that the mere functioning of the Japanese economic system was "by far the greatest contribution to the security of other countries in the East Asian Region." Japan's own "growth," its efficient structural adjustments to the oil crises of the 1970s, its movement towards higher technology industry, and its readiness to encourage other countries to pursue industrial development programs at lower levels of technology had helped to make possible economic successes and political stability/security elsewhere throughout the region. However, it was not easy, even for someone having access to IMF data, to prove that achievement statistically. Trade data and information on investment flows existed in profusion, but it was not obvious how they could be organized to demonstrate Japanese "causation": too many other factors were involved.

As to aid projects that gained for Japan conspicuous political capital, Saito observed for a start that Japan's dollar-denominated ODA commitments should help. Japan could build a second Panama Canal, and thus offer an example of high value/high "public attention" aid activity. High in cost, it would benefit a wide variety of users worldwide (see Appendix V).

Japan could not unilaterally, or even preeminently, make fundamental structural change in the international monetary system.

Saito's final comment: The assumed powers of the Japan discussed in the outline existed in a world economy which was growing: with low or even zero growth likely in Japan, and with continuing world depression, old notions of Japan's potentials could become irrelevant.

YOSHIO OKAWARA, AMBASSADOR
(January 4, 1983)

I talked with Yoshio Okawara, Japan's ambassador to the United States, shortly before my departure for Tokyo. His comments focused on several themes in my outline.

Everyone's security depended on improvement in the condition of the American economy: a serious and prolonged American depression would bring a worldwide economic crisis.

There was a fundamental difference in the framework within which Americans and Japanese discussed weapons. Washington's strategic concerns were global, and American comment on Japan's situation was always made in the global frame. Japan's own strategic calculations were made in a local frame, and thus affected the nature of Japan's self-defense efforts. These differences of perspective could create difficulty.

In discussing Japanese "intelligence" potentials there was danger of evoking images of the Soviet Committee for State Security (KGB) or of Japan's own prewar intelligence agencies; they were not attractive images. To link Japan's defense investment too closely with "intelligence" capability might not be wise.

On security matters, Southeast Asians remained sensitive and apprehensive about Japan's possible reemergence as a military power under pressure from the United States. It was important to probe carefully for real Southeast Asian commitment and expectation on security questions.

5
CONVERSATIONS
WITH SOME AMERICANS
IN GOVERNMENT AND BUSINESS

I have long known that sticking to the point can bleed an interview of what can be its most rewarding value — capturing some flavor of the man himself and profiting from his peripheral vision. From these Americans in government and business I got much more than flat replies to questions that my outline on "comprehensive security" provoked.

Taking off from the outline, Rubinstein drew upon his privileged positioning over many years, in Embassy Tokyo, in the Department of State, and at the Pentagon, to reveal how Americans and their Japanese counterparts thought differently about Japan's strategic role, and about specific ways that cooperative progress had been made. Auer's very close working relationship with the highest policy and negotiating levels of the Pentagon added particular interest to his assessment of Japan's dependence on the American nuclear umbrella. Auer was much in demand as lecturer and panelist on Pacific region security matters. An interview offers him opportunity, historically and analytically, to draw heavily and accurately on his participation in and knowledge of Washington's negotiations with Tokyo. I am indebted to Auer for acquainting me with Over the Horizon Radar (OTH) which may be a better investment than AWACS. From Armitage and Perle, I was given reminder that Pentagon planning seems to take place within a relatively brief time frame, and that Japan could construe "comprehensive security" appropriations to make possible strategic actions difficult for the United States to take (e.g., extending Japanese aid to Turkey, which the American Greek lobby would veto if attempted by the Pentagon).

Fei confirmed Japan's foreseeable preeminence worldwide in breeder reactor technology, recognized weapons proliferation potentials, and offered careful assessment of what difficulties Japan might encounter in lending support to new arms control arrangements. Recently, chairman of the Joint Chiefs of Staff (JCS), General David Jones saw merit in a Japanese investment in AWACS, especially if thought about metaphorically, but he believed that Japanese were much too sophisticated to attach magical properties to any military technology. He alluded to various surveillance technologies, especially for tracking submarines, and suspected that some very advanced technologies developed in the "European Theater" could be used for defense of Japan's straits/sea-lane approaches. It came as a surprise to me that General Jones had decided to use what influence he could exert to warn Americans about the great and dangerous consequences for the world of movement by the United States towards trade protectionism. Congressman James Jones shared that conviction. Going further, Jones expressed some mystification at racial overtones in trade balance-induced anti-Japanese sentiment. There might be no Japanese answer to free ride charges, he feared, short of paying heavily for weapons systems of other countries, including the United States. Erik Fromm provided me with much information about AWACS, which somehow escaped sounding like a Boeing sales pitch. When in Japan, I quoted him extensively, to the amazement of some Japanese whose interest in military build-up had not extended to details of surveillance technology.

GREGG RUBINSTEIN, DEPARTMENT OF DEFENSE (November 17, 1982)

Mr. Gregg Rubinstein was a proficient Japanese-speaking foreign service officer who had studied Japan's military establishment and its place in the Japanese system while on duty in the State Department, at the Pentagon, and at the American Embassy in Tokyo.

Rubinstein opened up his comments on the outline with the observation that the *Comprehensive National Security Report* stimulated, for a while, quite frequent use of that term in Washington. Americans seized upon the concept as a useful framework for suggesting cooperative approaches to mutual problems. However, as time passed, the Japanese seemed to be using the term almost exclusively to refer to nonmilitary activity. Tokyo seemed to assume that if Japan financed more ODA this justified financing less investment in defense. The Americans had hoped that there could be more financing of both, both being regarded as complementary. Washington seldom used the term anymore, fearing that doing so would be falling for a Japanese excuse for inaction.

Rubinstein elaborated at length about what Washington wanted Japan to do — for Japan itself, and for the United States — in the western Pacific. Japan's mission was seen to be defense of the home islands and surveillance of sea-lanes. The outline's formulation of the concepts of "knowledge is power" and "knowledge as deterrence" was useful and completely congenial, Rubinstein believed, to the Japanese mentality.

Rubinstein explained that BADGE (basic air defense ground environment) was the central knowledge-gathering and processing system that communicated with radar detection facilities reaching out to a radius of 200-300 miles. Japan's BADGE system was installed by Hughes in the 1960s, and was now being updated. Its sites were now being hardened. Its cryptographic capabilities were also being made more secure. With this as a start, joint conversations between Washington and Tokyo were heading in the direction of fleshing out some of the elements contained in the outline's "AWACS concept."

Washington was backing away from lobbying for increases above 1% of GNP as a measurement of Japanese defense performance. There was now more talk about qualitative improvement of Japan's military forces, and about missions.

Japan's E-2Cs — a radar-equipped aircraft with some of the capabilities of AWACS — were beginning to feed data into BADGE. Japan had Lockheed naval patrol aircraft, which were being used for antisubmarine surveillance. Japan also had some satellite capability — photographic, radar, and infrared — which until now had produced only fairly vague data. Other dimensions of intelligence gathering could include electronic surveillance (ELINT), which would make possible eavesdropping on communications to supplement information otherwise obtained. AWACS would supplement and extend Japan's knowledge of the environment, particularly of low-altitude enemy activity. However, Japan's immediate priorities should be completing its BADGE, E-2C, and P-3C programs.

These knowledge-gathering capabilities required the support of effective weapons systems. Japan's "defense-only" philosophy imposed limitations on weapon capabilities. For example, equipping Japan's F-4Es for bombing or in-flight refueling was taboo in the 1970s because such capabilities were construed as "offensive," but such interpretations had gradually changed. Japan now made the F-15, a longer-range, all-weather fighter with bombing and in-flight refueling capacity.

Were it accepted that combat engagement might take place as far away as Vladivostok and over the Northern Islands, these planes, working with U.S. forces and backed up by modern surface-to-air weapons (such as the new American PATRIOT missile), could cope with foreseeable requirements. To be effective, however, these systems must be supported by the improved BADGE, hardened airfields, and adequate supplies of fuel and munitions.

Similar concerns — that is, modernization and sustainability — also applied to Japan's Maritime and Ground Self Defense Forces. Japan's defense program was essentially in a training phase, procuring very high-quality equipment for high-quality personnel. It now needed to transform these elements into an effective military force within the framework of a more clearly articulated defense policy.

Another major issue was Japanese support of the U.S. military establishment in Japan. Actually, that support was already substantial. The United States used its base facilities without charge. Japan paid, in addition, a substantial share of operating costs for housing, labor, and facilities construction. Washington wanted Japan to further increase this contribution—in fact, ultimately, to support everything except American personnel and capital equipment.

Until three years ago, there was virtually no joint training or planning between the U.S. and Japanese military establishments. Considerable progress was now being made in this field and there had been substantial improvement in the scope and quality of joint exercises.

Japan's acquisition of U.S. defense equipment was a vital element in U.S.-Japanese security cooperation. Coproduction of such equipment by the Japanese was more expensive than off-the-shelf purchases from the U.S., but like many other countries Japan accepted some economic extravagance so as to strengthen, through acquisition of technology, its defense industrial base. Like other countries, Japan was, of course, interested in possible civilian applications of technology acquired through coproduction programs, though the implications of this interest remained unclear. The Pentagon must weigh these factors together with its strong interest in interoperability of equipment with its key Pacific ally in determining the trade-off between direct purchase or coproduction of U.S. equipment by Japan.

The prospect of turning defense technology transfers into a two-way process was a very significant development in U.S.-Japanese security relations. In May 1980, the Pentagon and the Japan Defense Agency (JDA) agreed to set up a Systems and Technology Forum (S&TF) to promote two-way collaboration in defense technology. Though there was little in current Japanese technology of interest to the United States, Washington hoped to establish a framework to facilitate contact between U.S. and Japanese industries and, upon mutual agreement, to permit the export of Japanese technology in the future.

Rubinstein went on to say that this promising initiative had encountered complications. The Japanese Ministry of International Trade and Industry (MITI) had thus far been reluctant to license defense-related exports, citing restrictions in a 1967 statute banning export of military equipment to Communist Bloc countries, to countries subjected to United Nations sanctions, and to countries engaged—or about to be engaged—in hostilities. In 1976, Prime Minister Miki's government expanded interpretation of the 1967 statute to make it apply to sales of all military-related items. (It was during Miki's tenure, Rubinstein recalled, that the 1% of GNP ceiling for military spending became enshrined as a principle of Japan's defense policy.)

Thus, the S&T Forum had produced quite disappointing results. Within Japan there were ongoing differences on how to handle cooperation in defense-related technology among the JDA (which obviously had the most to gain from such cooperation), the Foreign Ministry (which recognized the foreign policy desirability of transfers to the United States, but might be excessively bureaucratic in its approach to them), and MITI (which was charged with administering licenses, and resisted loss of administrative control while — rather ironically — professing concern over potential nondefense applications of Japanese technology exports to the United States). If there were no loosening on the Japanese side in the face of Washington's insistence on future reciprocity in technology transfers, the impact on future coproduction of defense equipment could be very serious. A failure to resolve the current problem of easing technology transfers would have a very undesirable impact upon implementing an "AWACS concept," further back-up of BADGE, a new satellite, and so forth. (In subsequent talks, Rubinstein noted that Prime Minister Nakasone's decision in January 1983 to allow the transfer to the United States of Japanese technology was a major step forward — but we would not know how far forward until specific agreements were negotiated.)

Rubinstein mentioned other important issues dealt with, or implicit in, the comprehensive security doctrine.

The roots of the three nuclear principles were deep and could be tampered with only at great political peril. This was evident during negotiation of the revised security treaty in 1960. Prime Minister Sato was only clarifying and reaffirming the principles in 1968, a process that had since continued. Sealane defense was not a U.S. idea. The Japanese Maritime Self Defense Force had been talking about it since the 1960s. Its views, refined by JDA civilians, lay in the background of Suzuki's 1981 commitment to look out for sea-lanes out to 1000 nautical miles.

Rubinstein said that since the middle of the nineteenth century Japan had been obsessed by its vulnerabilities and by the necessity of surviving in an unfriendly world. The response to this obsession over the past century had been varied — from Meiji Japan's feverish modernization of state and society, to prewar Japan's search for security through military domination of East Asia, and then to the postwar emphasis on trade expansion and international economic cooperation. The need to survive, however, had been a constant challenge, and given sufficient incentive, the method of responding to the challenge could change again.

COMMANDER JAMES AUER,
DEPARTMENT OF DEFENSE
(November 24, 1982)

Commander James E. Auer was principal action officer on Japan in the office of the assistant secretary of defense for international security affairs.

Conversant in Japanese, with degrees from Marquette and Tufts Universities, and stationed in Japan for many years, Auer was an extraordinarily well-informed and judicious analyst of U.S.-Japanese military relations.

Auer's views were as follows: My outline was extremely sympathetic to Japan. My outline failed, for example, to show that it was only the United States safety net that had given Japan the luxury of choice among a range of policy possibilities; much the same could be said, of course, about NATO. Many presumed Japanese options would be simply impractical were it not that Japan enjoyed a U.S. guarantee.

Japan would, itself, have to decide how to play a role in its own defense. Effective defense might not be possible at all without the protection of a nuclear umbrella. Neither Tokyo nor Washington wanted Japan, itself, to have nuclear weapons. In that sense, Japan's military role would necessarily be limited.

Japan's security doctrine had evolved by stages. In 1956 Japan published its basic statement on self-defense policy, declaring, in doing so, intention to show good will towards all countries, to cooperate with the United Nations, to build effective self-defense gradually, and to respect its security treaty with the United States. A restatement — the *National Defense Program Outline* — was issued in 1976, but scheduled achievement of its basic goal of effective self defense had never been met.

After the Soviet invasion of Afghanistan in 1979, the Carter administration placed heavy pressure on Japan to indicate disapproval. During the 1970s, Japan's real annual increases in defense spending had been about 7.8%. Secretary Brown stated this was insufficient, and Prime Minister Ohira stated he would seek to do more. A ceiling of 9.7% in nominal terms (about 6% real) was set for fiscal year (FY) 1981, but the Japanese government decided, at the end of 1980, on only a 7.6% nominal increase.

This had been the backdrop for commencement of the Reagan administration's talks about defense matters with Tokyo. As to style, Secretary of State Haig chose to handle defense matters with all allies, including Japan, in private, rather than through public proclamation or criticism. He also discounted the importance of dwelling on "percentage of GNP" as the most useful measure of commitment. Both Haig and Secretary of Defense Weinberger focused on missions, burden sharing, and real effectiveness of forces. This was the approach underlying Weinberger's March 1981 talks with Japan's Foreign Minister in Washington and the Reagan-Suzuki summit in May. The summit's joint communiqué endorsed a division of labor but left its terms unspecified. In response to a question at the Press Club, however, Suzuki went further, saying it was consistent with Japan's Constitution to defend its own territory and waters out to 1000 nautical miles and that such was Japan's policy. There was, subsequently, confusion over the reach of that commitment. Japanese-U.S. measurement was from Osaka to north of the

Philippines, and from Tokyo to Guam. Many Southeast Asians, anxiously, measured from other points in Japan.

Six months into the Reagan administration, the U.S.-Japanese Security Subcommittee met in Hawaii. Japanese press reports indicated that the United States presented its estimate of what was needed to carry out the Suzuki policy—in terms of ammunition and additional naval and air capabilities. Foreign Minister Sonoda characterized this presentation as "demands," and the Suzuki response was evasive.

In March 1982, Weinberger visited Tokyo. He described the Soviet military build-up, and press reports stated that the secretary recommended that Japan speed up achieving the goals it had set for itself. These reports claimed that he stated that doing this by 1990 would require real budget increases at a rate of 10% annually in real terms, and that a 1982 nominal 7.7% increase would represent only a 4% real increase. The press accounts said these recommendations would bring Japanese military spending to 1.8% of GNP in 1991. Suzuki was reported to have asked experts to review such matters at the next Security Subcommittee meeting.

At the end of August 1982, the Security Subcommittee met again in Hawaii. The Japanese side presented Japan's five-year defense plan. The United States presented its views on defense of sea-lanes, at the request of Minister of Defense Ito.

The atmosphere of discussions was excellent. However, Japan's plan represented an intention to achieve no more than the force levels contained in the 1976 *National Defense Program Outline,* an outdated analysis that contained no realistic provision for ammunition stocks or for sufficient aircraft and ship procurement for the sea-lane mission. This was not a Japan Defense Agency plan: it seemed to be what the Ministry of Finance would allow the agency to submit.

The American critique was forthright: By 1990 Japan would not be able to defend itself. Japan could not defend its sea-lanes out 1000 nautical miles. Japan would be more vulnerable, owing to demands on U.S. resources in other danger areas. The Japanese proposed creation of a Joint Study Group to consider the problem further.

Meanwhile, the 1983 ceiling for increase in defense spending was still standing at a nominal 7.3%, or a real 4%. (The final figure was subsequently set at 6.5% nominal.)

Auer credited the Foreign Ministry with readiness to press for greater Japanese defense spending. Slow movement could not fairly be attributed to negative public opinion. Low rates of spending had to be attributed to the political and bureaucratic power of the Ministry of Finance.

Some, it was true, attributed spending restraint to fear that militarization would cause a surge toward military extremism. However, Japan's left wing was relatively impotent and had been rendered even more so with Chinese endorsement of the U.S.-Japanese Security Treaty and Japan's defense build-up. Thus, according to Auer, it was the United States military presence in Japan that obviated the need for Japan to build up its own forces so greatly as to thrust the military extremists closer to power. Withdrawal of the American presence, and not Japanese burden sharing, was what might cause a Japanese swing to the right.

There were specific military tasks. Japan should improve its leaky air defenses. It should build up to at least 60-day ammunition stocks (they were now four to five days). Japan should extend the reach of early warning, in part because numbers of Soviet aircraft were much larger than recently expected and would rise. Japan should game out tactics to use in sea-lane protection. Doing such things could help to silence congressional dissatisfaction with Japan's military role.

There was appeal, Auer said, in my "AWACS concept," but OTH (Over the Horizon Radar) might be an even better investment, considering Japan's earlier commitment to acquire the E-2C. With OTH, you saw nothing for 500 miles, but for 1000-2000 miles beyond you saw "something there," thus gaining time to perfect knowledge as the activity drew nearer. OTH had attractive features. It was an old technology and relatively inexpensive. Its critical elements could be easily and effectively hardened. Its vulnerable elements, if knocked out, were replaceable easily and at low cost. And although radar information was vague, use of computers could give it greater precision.

RICHARD ARMITAGE, DEPARTMENT OF DEFENSE
(December 30, 1982)

Richard Armitage was the highly regarded deputy assistant secretary of defense for international security affairs. He had frequently represented the United States in negotiations with Japanese authorities on security matters. He offered suggestive comment on how "comprehensive security" could affect his negotiating tactics.

There were many attractive ways for Japan to build up what would be some really increased defense capability. As one possibility, AWACS did have some appeal, but to go down that path might use up a year's appropriations. And there were more urgent needs. It would be better to use the E-2C, as planned, and put money saved in more immediately usable war-fighting equipment and stocks (i.e., ammunition and spare parts). Pentagon planning for establishing priorities in procurement, burden sharing, and roles and missions fell within a time frame reaching to the end of this decade, which, for a military establishment, was not a long time.

RICHARD PERLE, DEPARTMENT OF DEFENSE
(January 4, 1983)

Richard Perle was currently assistant secretary of defense for international security policy. Formerly an aide to Senator Jackson, he was now regarded as a brilliant Reagan administration "insider" of extreme anti-Soviet persuasion. Perle commented on the United States-Japan relationship.

It was bad tactics, he believed, to focus on getting Japan merely to increase defense spending. Japan's comprehensive security concept was entirely sound.

Japan should contribute to mutual security in other ways than merely arms build-up; there were many projects Japan could undertake, in the common interest, that the United States itself could not take on, aid for example to Turkey (we had a Greek lobby, and Japan did not).

As to my "AWACS concept," Perle said that he had been exploring AWACS' worldwide potentials, within which a Japanese contribution would have great value. In any case, he seemed to say, the Japanese concept opened up promising possibilities for dealing with security problems other than by just acquiring weapons.

EDWARD FEI, ARMS CONTROL
AND DISARMAMENT AGENCY
(December 1, 1982)

Edward Fei was, at the time of our conversation, a senior Far Eastern specialist in the United States Arms Control and Disarmament Agency. I asked him to speculate, in a personal capacity, about how Japan's huge investment in nuclear power capability might contribute to regional arms control arrangements.

Fei doubted that other East Asian countries would wish to become closely associated with Japan's efforts to master nuclear power technology in the near future. He mentioned several reasons: the economic orientation of nations such as South Korea and Taiwan towards the United States and their ties to the U.S. nuclear establishment; the use of English as the international language of science; and sharp memories of Japan's behavior in World War II which caused many countries to prefer a partnership with the United States to one with Japan.

In the past, South Korea and Taiwan had relied almost exclusively on the United States for technology and training and had no history of technological cooperation with Japan. Japan was advancing its own R and D, but had not produced any of its own reactors. Taiwan and South Korea viewed Japan more as a competitor than as a substitute for the United States.

Fei offered as a possible model for regional nuclear cooperation Joseph Yager's concept of a Far Eastern "EURATOM," (European Atomic Energy Commission), a group of nations that could negotiate with the United States as a bloc rather than individually. Such a collective agency could offer benefits to all involved. For the United States, benefits would be administrative. South Korea and Taiwan might obtain some benefits that Japan already had. Japan, already being the dominant member of any such bloc, would have greater access to Korean and Taiwanese nuclear industries commercially and might give reassurance that the intent of their nuclear programs remained peaceful. At present, the United States knew more than Japan about what was going on in these countries. Still to be contended with, however, would be the traditional dislike of the Koreans for the Japanese.

As to the possibility of multinational arrangements for reprocessing reactor fuel, the United States itself did not reprocess light water reactor fuel, only stored it, because the process was difficult, was costly, and required special facilities and handling. Only England and France had done such reprocessing, but they had, now, no excess storage capacity or ability to take orders. Despite the argument advanced by some countries that reprocessing might be a useful waste management tool, the United States itself preferred to store fuel rods (which contained plutonium and other radioactive substances). Storage was cheaper than reprocessing. The United States did not believe that reprocessing of power reactor fuel was the best course for South Korea and Taiwan.

Meanwhile, the Japanese had built a pilot reprocessing center, Tokaimura, using French technology. Now the Japanese wanted to build a larger facility. The Japanese were keenly aware of the problems, but they wanted to reprocess because Japan might have the world's most urgent problem with waste disposal: Japan had no interest in weapons materials. Reprocessing produced large amounts of its own waste — in addition to tons of plutonium — but much was low-level. The Japanese had considered dumping some low level wastes in the ocean.

Actually, Washington would favor an international reprocessing center, located perhaps in Japan, but domestic Japanese opposition to spent fuel storage and reprocessing would be even higher than at present if the waste came from other countries. Furthermore, in Japan, utility companies managed spent fuel, and from their standpoint an international reprocessing center in Japan would only compound their waste disposal problems. A more effective approach might be to discuss the possibility with the Japanese defense and/or foreign policy establishments, which might view Japanese participation in regional reprocessing with Korea or Taiwan as beneficial to regional stability and national security.

Japan's commitment to breeder reactors was shown in the scale of its investment and in R and D, but there would be problems. They had a prototype, the Joyo Fast Breeder Reactor. (The French had two, the Phoenix and the Super Phoenix.) These breeder reactors were discussed in Yager's books.

The Reagan administration came into office believing that the United States government had, in the past, been unproductively rigid on nonproliferation. The administration's present policy was not to inhibit reprocessing by Western Europe or by Japan. The United States trusted the effectiveness of its tight system of controls on our fuels and technology, which applied to retransfer, explosive use, reprocessing, and storage by others. Any such "subsequent arrangements" would require U.S. approval.

As to Japan's nuclear power role in Southeast Asia, the Philippines and Indonesia had made significant investments in nuclear power, and might also join Taiwan and South Korea in some kind of broader international scheme. Japan might consider helping along such a project, but these countries would probably prefer dealing with the United States — the leader in nuclear technology, and, in the case of the Philippines, historically an ally. Even if the Philippines were tempted to explore cooperation with Japan, Japan was not producing reactors, so the Philippines could not get them there. In general, however, Southeast Asia did not now offer much of a market for reactors.

Discussing the future of nuclear power in the United States, Fei commented that he was struck by the publication of an article in the *Washington Post* written by a managing director of the Tennessee Valley Authority. The article said that the American light-water reactors had problems, in part because they were produced before anyone had actual long-term experience with their operation.[9] Fei believed that the Japanese, skilled at handling detail, might be as good or better at operating reactors than Americans. Currently, the U.S. reactor market was stagnant, and orders were being cancelled. Only Japan, Korea, and Taiwan were likely to be buying reactors.

Asked about "first use," Fei, referring to the position taken by Messrs. Bundy, McNamara, Smith, and Kennan, pointed out that China had already taken a "no first use" stand. The Japanese seemed, however, to have viewed this issue as irrelevant to their situation. The U.S.-U.S.S.R. nuclear arms race was, for Japan, a sort of "invisible problem."

GENERAL DAVID JONES,
FORMER CHAIRMAN, JOINT CHIEFS OF STAFF
(December 7, 1982)

I told General David C. Jones, recent chairman of the Joint Chiefs of Staff, that I had come to believe that there was great need to help Japan to talk more, and more convincingly, about its present and potential contributions to mutual security, so as to reduce hostile "free ride" charges of critical congressmen, without, in doing so, reviving in Japan's East Asian neighborhood ugly memories of Japanese militarism. The "AWACS concept" was my "magical formula." What, I asked, was wrong with it?

Jones liked the formula, but cited difficulties. First, AWACS, though expensive, (and therefore helpful in closing the trade deficit) was not as expensive as I suggested. The Saudis' $8 billion tab meant that the AWACS package contained much that Japan would not need. Second, AWACS might be "magical" in some places, but probably not in Japan: they knew too much for "magic." Third, Japan had already analyzed the merits of AWACS and the E-2C, and decided on the E-2C: to now embrace AWACS would mean awkward admission of earlier miscalculation.

Still, AWACS was well worth advocating, particularly if talked about metaphorically. For example, if the mission of surveillance were widened to include land and sea, AWACS would be much better. If surveillance were continuous and not intermittent, AWACS would be less expensive. E-2C was less expensive per aircraft, but more expensive to operate on a continuous orbit at considerable distance. The United States had AWACS in Okinawa, for Korea-oriented reasons. For Japan to have AWACS, for example, in Hokkaido and Kyushu might be very desirable, but for what specific mission had not yet been articulated. Whether AWACS and E-2C could be combined usefully would, again, depend on what came to be the definition of their respective missions.

Jones liked my "AWACS concept" but suspected that Japan's decision to buy the E-2C had undercut it. A larger concept might be better. As to my own larger concept, I explained that it was to come up with a "defense only" military capability that would result from mobilization of Japan's genius in electronics, computers, engineering, and "high tech," and that would have undeniable combat potential against the Soviet Union but would not alarm friends. Suzuki's 1000 nautical mile defense commitment did not seem to be meeting that standard. Jones agreed.

As to improved surveillance, Jones made comment. Some thought it required many more surface craft, destroyers, and so forth: he would not favor a much larger investment in such craft. Actually, American capabilities in these categories were already excellent, and quite capable of coping with Soviet ships in the same categories.

Submarines were the great threat. Japan's investment in P-3 aircraft (Navy antisubmarine warfare — ASW) was sensible and fulfilled the surveillance function more efficiently than surface craft, especially if they were armed with Harpoon. There were, in addition, many other effective technologies for submarine tracking, the P-3, with its capability of dropping sonic devices that could pick up "signatures" of enemy submarines being only one. There could be tracking by surface warships, also with their sonic devices. There was underwater submarine tracking of submarines. Jones spoke highly of technology used with great success in the Atlantic, down a trough from Iceland south. Jones believed that only limited use had been made of some of these "European Theater" technologies in the Pacific. Some of them might be appropriate for Japan's home island/Sea of Japan needs, even though the cost would be high.

I asked Jones if electromagnetic pulse (EMP) did not make informed nuclear war-making impossible. The threat of EMP to security/operability of communications was, Jones acknowledged, serious, and communications-command-control and intelligence (CCC and I) was given the highest priority by the United States. E-4, the government's most sophisticated airborne command center, was hardened for EMP.

I asked Jones whether or not EMP made risks of using strategic nuclear weapons unacceptable. He replied that EMP could "knock out" some communications, and might paralyze functioning of much of command and control facilities for a time, but probably not paralyze all of them for a very long time.

I recalled that some years back nuclear-weapons strategists attached importance to exchanges of knowledge between adversaries, even while nuclear engagement was under way. Only thus could escalation and, in eventual effect, risk of human extermination, be controlled: if EMP rendered one side or the other blind, was not there near certainty of mindless rage on the part of field commanders, and real holocaust? Jones discounted my fear of the breakdown of discipline, even if there were loss of communication links with command headquarters, which would produce "mindless rage." Jones added, however, that we were dealing with a heavy subject, which could occupy our time for the rest of the day.

Jones approved undertaking a project intended to persuade members of the Japanese Diet to do more about mutual security, and to persuade members of the American Congress that Japan was, in fact, doing more than they realized. He told me that he had considered it important to join a group — including former Secretary of the Treasury William Simon — dedicated to forestalling U.S. movement towards trade protectionism, a disease that could have dangerous consequences for the world.

CONGRESSMAN JAMES JONES, CHAIRMAN, HOUSE BUDGET COMMITTEE (December 21, 1982)

Congressman James Jones (Oklahoma), chairman of the powerful House Budget Committee, considered the outline good, innovative, and provocative. He had studied it, and would offer no dissents. However, he had been particularly struck by the chapter on Japan as a nuclear power. He had not, he said, given much thought to implications of Japan's nuclear power-generating capabilities. It would have growing general importance, particularly in the next generation. And never far from our minds should be the possibility that Japan could be driven, perhaps irrationally, towards acquiring nuclear weapons.

Jones reported that he had become more and more concerned about the growing virulence of anti-Japanese feeling in this country. For some time, he had believed those feelings were motivated by envy, fear of Japan's competitive powers, and other "civilized" forms of prejudice. However, he now detected, with alarm, disturbing evidence of racial dislike. He could not be sure about the origin of such feelings, but perhaps they went back to World War II. His anxiety was reinforced when he observed usually muted "racial" prejudice showing even in the language and behavior of ASEAN countries.

Japan was, of course, and should be, deeply concerned. As an insular country it suffered natural fear of being isolated. Though its situation was, of course, entirely different from that of the Soviet Union, both seemed to have paranoiac inclinations. That state of mind enhanced risks for everyone.

The outline suggested that Japan invest in a high-performance AWACS system. This was innovative and appealing. To acquire that high-cost, "defense only" capability might reduce American "free ride" charges. However, acquiring AWACS would not resolve all problems. Washington might worry about Japan's having its own independent intelligence-gathering capability. In exchange for AWACS, Washington might insist that Tokyo share with Washington the technological improvements/accessories Japan developed. The project might fail unless the United States and Japan entered into *joint* commitment and genuine sharing. For Japan to play a preeminent role in Northeast Asia, intelligence gathering and processing could be of great value, but Japan should go that way as a real partner, ready to share with the United States improvements achieved in the development of its own AWACS. Otherwise, the venture might have some negative results.

Jones discounted the relevance of Article 9 in Tokyo's strategic calculations. He did not discount the reality of Japanese sensitivity over any drift towards militarism. However, Japanese sensitivities over defense issues were, he believed, less raw than sensitivity to issues involving agriculture.

The answer to "free ride" by picking up more of defense costs might have to come in the form of Japanese financial support of the weapons systems of other countries and in greater cash payments to the United States for important weapons and military capabilities that Japan itself would not want.

Jones said that he would like to think that the Japanese assessment of the Soviet threat was not unrealistic. During January he would go to Moscow to form an opinion of his own.

ERIK FROMM, BOEING
(November 23, 1982)

Erik Fromm was a policy analyst and writer for Boeing. I asked him to tell me what he could about the cost, capabilities, politics, and deployment of the AWACS system. Boeing, Fromm explained, was the prime contractor and system integrator for USAF E-3 (AWACS). Also, Boeing produced the AWACS frame. Westinghouse produced the surveillance radar, International Business Machines (IBM) the data processing hardware, and many other suppliers provided the equipment AWACS carried.

There were almost thirty AWACS (of the planned thirty-four) in operation by the U.S. Air Force. They were deployed in Iceland, Alaska, the continental United States, and Okinawa, with a few moving in and out of Korea, West Germany, the Middle East, and parts of the NATO areas. None was in France. A continuous station orbit had been maintained in the Arabian Gulf area since October 1980 at the request of the Saudi Arabian government. In 1983, a contract was signed for a force of five AWACS plus tankers with the Saudi government. The Saudi AWACS would be deployed starting in 1985. These were part of a very large Saudi air-defense build-up with a price tag of about $5.6 billion, but the price could creep up to $8 billion because the package included F-15s, air-to-air missiles, conformal tanks, ground CCC facilities ($3 billion), tankers (six or eight), and training and logistical support. Unit cost of the AWACS alone came to about $80 million per copy. Also Boeing was currently delivering AWACS to NATO for its advanced early warning (AEW) aircraft; seven of the eighteen aircraft ordered had been delivered.

The idea of a Japan-based AWACS was not new. There were friends of the project in Congress, in the Pentagon, in the Department of State, in the National Security Council (NSC), and elsewhere. No one in Washington was opposed to Japanese possession of AWACS, but the project did not now have one compulsive advocate. Rather, the United States was waiting for the Japanese to select their operational AEW.

The Japanese considered AWACS in 1977 for the MIG-25 threat and selected the less capable E-2C. Oddly, this was done *because* AWACS had command and control (i.e., "battle-management") capability, and because the E-2C had a *shorter* range: these negative judgments were based on Japan's "defense only" principles.

Japan's decision to acquire Grumman's E-2Cs would give four to Japan in 1983, four in 1985, and one post-1985. Actually, AWACS was a better force multiplier. It had a 10.5-hour flight capability — or much longer, if refueled — compared to 5 hours for the E-2Cs. E-2C radar was more easily jammable. AWACS 1000-mile coverage assured more warning time for Backfire air-to-surface missile (ASM) launching (which could be 150 miles out). AWACS radar would pick up all surface ships and aircraft, over all terrains, and in the Straits areas. It would not pick up ground movement at less than eight knots velocity.

AWACS' links with its ground facilities, or the expected upgraded BADGE, would make possible constant communication to the ground of radar information, communication of that information to other aircraft, some

ELINT, and, in combination with other information-gathering facilities, would make possible retrieval of photographic, cryptographic, acoustic, and electronic information fed to the computer system. Thus would be created the "battle-management" capability.

Satellite tie-in would enhance the value of AWACS, but satellites were vulnerable to weather, might not be in the right place, and their infrared technology was slow.

Supporters of an Air Force AWACS were not opposed to the Navy's E-2C. Their technologies and operations complemented each other. In view of serious deficiencies in Japan's present system of interservice cooperation, Japan should be interested in greatly improved interservice cooperation inherent in functioning of the AWACS CCC and I, particularly tying in maritime (P-3Cs), etc., with air self-defense forces (F-15) for example.

Three AWACS for Japan would be cost-effective. Ten would meet most of the air-defense and sea-lane surveillance requirements. It would be best to have them tied to a single base area, which should not be located in a high threat locality. For $1 billion, ten AWACS might be put in business between 1984 and 1986.

The Russians had their Soviet-made AWACS—the MOSS—but it was a primitive version of the American AWACS. An improved second generation was in sight, apparently employing the overland look-down air target-detection capabilities of the E-3 AWACS.

6
CONVERSATIONS IN WASHINGTON WITH SOME AMERICAN "INSIDERS"

Neither in Tokyo nor in any European capital can there be found that easy, lateral professional mobility that makes it possible for members of an American public affairs elite in search of fame, power, and affluence—or even mere public service—to glide from universities into bureaucracies, into the media, or into business before returning to some comfortably familiar base of operations to "operate." George Ball, as former undersecretary of state, as investment banker, as author of many books of great stylistic elegance, and as "moral counselor" through editorial columns in many periodicals and journals, set a high standard for such participation in the nation's policy process by private persons. Ball was role model for many who aspired to be "insiders" though outside of government. Michael Blumenthal, Robert Roosa, Walter Heller, General Maxwell Taylor, Henry Kissinger, and many others were models of the same kind. Such outside insiders need not be famous or rich. However, as "insiders" they must know where power resides in the American system. Through the written word or by testimony offered at congressional hearings, on radio and television talk shows, or elsewhere, they know how to speak astutely as outsiders with the vocabulary and instinct for relevance of the real insiders.

I.M. Destler has written, in recent years, with a sure touch about U.S.-Japanese trade relations. His acerbic comment on "comprehensive security" reflected trepidation that Japan was unlikely to answer charges of "free ride" merely by rhetoric, or even by substantial performance, unnoticed because Japanese have no talent for self-congratulation.

Many years of distinguished academic achievement at Harvard, Columbia, the University of Hawaii, and Johns Hopkins, many years of service as foreign correspondent for the Associated Press, as *Washington Post* bureau chief in New Delhi and Tokyo, as managing editor of the *New Republic,* and as author of the widely translated *The Widening Gulf* went into Selig Harrison's readiness to understand and to make efforts to explain Japan's unwillingness to accept, without question, American premises in talk about such security matters as "free ride," burden sharing, and "integration" of military planning. There was logic and litigimacy, Harrison suggested, in Japan's desire to make its own autonomous judgments.

Richard Solomon, author of a recent Rand Corporation study on *Asian Security in the 1980s,* long-time China watcher at Ann Arbor, and collaborator wth Henry Kissinger at the NSC, rightly noted insufficient attention being paid to the China variable in Japan's calculations on security matters. He doubted that Japan could quantify very impressively its use of nonmilitary instruments for security purposes. He did not rule out the possibility that Nakasone would try to loosen Japan's three nuclear principles. He saw desirable potentials in enlargement of two-way technology transfers.

Barry Blechman, on the faculty at Georgetown University's Center for Strategic and International Studies, one of the drafters of the Olof Palme Commission's disarmament report, a former senior staff member of the State Department's Arms Control and Disarmament Agency and the Carnegie Endowment for International Peace, and author of a major study of the Japanese defense establishment for Senator Glenn and the Senate Foreign Relations Committee, had read the outline. He was inclined to see it as too forgiving to Tokyo.

William Watts' close links with the White House, the executive and legislative branches, and the media and universities, over many years, had offered him occasion to sort out how Japan was viewed differently from these various points of view.

Admiral Noel Gayler's previous command of the U.S. forces in the Pacific lent authority to his skepticism about use of destroyers for antisubmarine warfare, and to his realization that investment in intelligence had high cost-effectiveness.

As principal economic reporter for the *Washington Post,* and with a flair for identifying sensitive public issues early in their gestation, Hobart Rowen drew attention to growing American anxiety that Japan's miltary build-up might offer Japanese industry the occasion for acquisition of high technology usable in its already highly competitive industry, but otherwise not available to it.

Richard Barnet's career had taken him into government service, administration of a research foundation, and a prolific output of books and articles on a wide variety of public policy issues. Throughout, arms control and East-West relations have been continuing preoccupations. Japan's concept of comprehensive security captured Barnet's particular interest because in that concept he found definitions of objective that should be embraced by Washington.

I.M. DESTLER,
INSTITUTE FOR INTERNATIONAL ECONOMICS
(November 23, 1982)

I.M. Destler, a senior associate of the Institute for International Economics, was a celebrated analyst of executive-legislative branch relationships in the conduct of foreign policy who was often asked to write or to appear on television to discuss U.S.-Japanese relations.

Destler's simple answer to the question of how to silence American charges of "free ride" was for Japan to spend more on Japan's military establishment and for Japan to give more aid to the region. "Free ride" charges might never be silenced with finality, but there probably had to be a somewhat larger military effort, and a commitment to protect effectively the Japanese islands. The question was whether even a large increase in Japan's defense spending could appear sufficient to American writers. Did we know that a Japan spending 1.5% or 2% of GNP on defense, for example, would look significantly better to American critics (in relation to our 6% or 7%)?

As hinted at in the *Comprehensive Security Report,* Japan could come up with an alternative to American definitions of what was required to achieve security. This was, Destler believed, potentially a promising idea: a broader conception would appeal to Americans and Europeans who felt that Washington currently overemphasized the military dimension. However, a Japanese alternative would have to be concrete enough to escape accusation that it was merely a dodge—an evasion of responsibility.

As to making AWACS the matrix of a "defense only" doctrine, there were difficulties. The AWACS capability could be regarded by some of Japan's neighbors as intrusive. As to ODA, Japan had increased such resource transfers more rapidly, perhaps, than others. Doing this, however, had not produced any major political spin-off. Moreover, much Japanese ODA was viewed skeptically as being tied and therefore self-serving. As to the yen-dollar rate, and the international monetary system, reform could bring very large returns in rectifying trade imbalances and dampening U.S. protectionism. But Japan alone could not, according to Destler, achieve these reforms.

Japan should, of course, ponder possibilities for promising new financial and commercial strategies. However, inherent in the Japanese culture was reluctance to advance new ideas—much less to exhort others to carry forward with them.

SELIG HARRISON,
CARNEGIE ENDOWMENT
FOR INTERNATIONAL PEACE
(November 24, 1982)

Selig Harrison, currently a Senior Associate of the Carnegie Endowment, said that the structure of the outline was stimulating, especially in indicating the need for fresh approaches to the question of Japan's role in the Pacific region. On specifics, the "AWACS concept," being clearly for defense only, was attractive. The ASEAN Coast Guard was also a constructive notion. And the thought that Japan could take a bold stand on the "no first use" issue had intriguing, possibly constructive implications for future U.S.-Japanese military cooperation.

With respect to the "burden-sharing" issue, Harrison said that Japanese and American perceptions clashed. As many Americans saw it, the United States showed rare benevolence in helping a defeated enemy to its feet, and the affluent Japan of the 1980s should feel indebted for past assistance as well as for its continuing military "free ride." This view held that Japan could never have achieved its "economic miracle" without American loan capital and technical help, not to mention Japanese earnings from the Korean and Vietnam Wars. In Japan, however, this concept of a "debt" was flatly rejected, since most Japanese believed that the United States rebuilt Japan for its own strategic reasons as an industrial bulwark against the Soviet Union and China.

In Japanese eyes the postwar "miracle" was a natural outgrowth of the progress Japan had achieved on its own before the war. This progress was attributed to many of the same factors typically cited by foreign observers — a unified social structure unique in Asia, a driving nationalism, and a disciplinarian work ethic. These were the all-important qualities that, to the Japanese, explained why they were able to make more effective use of the cold-war dollars flowing their way than most other Asian countries.

Despite continuing domestic opposition to the Japan-United States security treaty, successive conservative Japanese regimes had been able to sustain their "special relationship" with the United States by presenting it as a trade-off in which Tokyo had provided military privileges and foreign policy support in exchange for American solicitude in economic matters. For many of the ruling conservatives themselves, the treaty had had a specifically military rationale. But for the broader Japanese public, with its diversity of foreign policy views, the alliance had been politically digestible in economic terms.

Most Japanese had viewed the treaty as a tacit precondition for assuring access to the American market as well as for securing stable supplies of food grains and a variety of American, or American-controlled, natural resources, notably oil, enriched uranium, and coking coal (see Appendix I).

Increasingly in recent years the dynamics of the trade-off had been changing. The economic benefits resulting from the American connection, while still substantial, were reaching a plateau in some areas and slowly tapering off in others. Protectionism in Washington was likely to limit the future growth of Japanese exports to the American market. Tokyo no longer saw its dependence on the Western oil companies as uniformly advantageous and had been systematically shifting to direct dealings with producer countries.

This change in the trade-off, according to Harrison, had made Tokyo less willing than ever to accede to "burden-sharing" pressures, and such pressures could be counterproductive, undermining the security treaty itself. Americans who advocated "integration" of U.S.-Japanese military planning were on the wrong track. Japan's desire for autonomy should be respected.

In the economic field, Japan could contribute to shared American and Japanese goals of economic development through economic aid and liberal export credit terms for developing countries. Harrison stressed that Japanese corporations were more flexible than their American counterparts in working with public sector industrial enterprises in developing countries. As an example of a Japanese *private* enterprise joining in a successful joint venture with a *governmental* enterprise, he pointed to the Indian government's Maruti joining with Suzuki (49%) in the production of cars and scooters. Such arrangements effected technology transfers in an efficient way.

Japan's ODA should, of course, be increased, even if it involved more tied aid.

RICHARD SOLOMON, RAND CORPORATION
(December 15, 1982)

Richard Solomon said that the outline was a good way to move in on serious problems, particularly with its allusions to Southeast Asia. However, there had to be some real question about the comprehensive security concept and Japan's motive in formulating it. Was it mere rationalization for inactivity in building up military defenses? Was it a way of justifying self-serving economic investment that would facilitate market development? Was it a ploy supposed to please Americans?

If downgrading investment in weapons was to be explained by commitment to make greater use of nonmilitary instruments, what numbers could be presented to show actual performance? Japan's ODA did not look particularly impressive. How could sharing of Japan's knowledge and technology with others be quantified? Unless these data existed and could be persuasively presented, the charge of "free ride" would continue, Solomon feared, to have some real justification.

Solomon asked me what basis there really was for saying that Tokyo and Washington viewed the reality of a Sino-Soviet bloc differently back in the 1950s. I replied that Japan's declared intention to separate politics from economics, even during the Korean War, seemed to flow from real differences in Japan's and our attitudes towards all Communist countries. Solomon believed that Tokyo was now carefully watching trends in the Moscow-Peking connection: eternal split could not be taken for granted. If rapprochement became more likely, Tokyo might not want to remain totally dependent for its security on Washington — or, contrariwise, of course, it could "lean" more heavily on the United States (i.e., move back a bit from China and be more apprehensive about the Soviets).

Solomon himself seriously doubted that even some defrosting in Moscow-Peking relations would alter Soviet involvement in the Vietnam/Kampuchea situation, or reduce Moscow's military investment in the Northern Islands. However, Moscow might redeploy some forces away from the Chinese border. If Peking viewed this with too great relief, Washington and Tokyo, too, could come to look differently at China's helpful potentials in the East Asian strategic configuration.

Japan's way of assessing the Soviet threat had, without doubt, been influenced over the years by its great confidence in the American commitment to confront Soviet military potentials in Northeast Asia. Solomon believed that mounting evidence that American military resources might, in time of need, be sent to Southwest Asia had begun to cause the Japanese to recalculate, independently, their own security needs. For Japan to invest more in modernization of its military establishment — "for defense only" — within the context of the security treaty, would be of real help to the United States, and should mute charges of "free ride."

As to my "AWACS concept," Solomon said that it would be very helpful in enabling us to deal with the growing Backfire bomber threat, but that the American military was "goosey" about ever depending on other people's intelligence for its operations.

Technological exchanges between the Japanese and Americans had obviously desirable potentials. Solomon saw Japan's genius as strong in applications rather than in basic innovation. Even so, Japan had much to share with us. MITI was a real obstacle, given its interest in preserving Japan's trading advantages, but there was recent improvement in arrangements from which both sides should profit.

Solomon wondered if Nakasone might not try to alter Japan's 3 nuclear principles to "2½" — by accepting transit arrangements more openly.

BARRY BLECHMAN, CENTER FOR STRATEGIC AND INTERNATIONAL STUDIES OF GEORGETOWN UNIVERSITY
(December 2, 1982)

Barry Blechman disliked what he perceived as my overly sympathetic treatment of Japan's security policies and behavior in the outline. Japan's doctrines, he believed, were largely an excuse for inactivity, rather than a truly coherent rationale for preserving national and regional security. The outline had understated, in addition, the legitimacy of Washington's concern about the undeniable inadequacy of Japan's contribution to mutual security requirements in the region.

Blechman noted allusion in the outline to Japan's declared intent to compensate for low spending on the military establishment by using "nonmilitary instruments." The fact was that Japan's record in using such "instruments" was quite poor when compared, for example, with that of the Federal Republic of Germany.

As to "threats," there was, again, a pro-Japanese bias. There was implication of uncertainty and distrust in the American nuclear umbrella. There was also implication of uncertainty in retaining access to the American market.

Blechman said that it might be true, and probably was, that Japan did poorly in keeping its books so as to gain full credit for helpful aid programs. It would be wise, however, to document that assertion. I responded that both at the State Department and at the Pentagon Japan's aid to Egypt, Turkey, and Pakistan had been praised, even though these programs were largely ignored in the Japanese media, and even in official documentation. I surmised that Tokyo might want to do much more, as a practical matter, than it wanted to have reviewed by the Diet.

Blechman concurred in much that the outline covered on "knowledge as deterrence." There should be a more convincing explanation of capability to deny the Soviet navy use of the Straits. Japan should think about the control of Japan's air space, not only to defend Japan, but also to lend operational support as necessary and possible to the needs of American forces in the area. Antisubmarine activity also should have that broader purpose.

Japan's R and D and high-tech missions should contribute to U.S. needs. And, where strategy and economics intersected or overlapped, Japan should take proper account of the fact that purchase of American equipment would help to narrow bilateral balance-of-payment deficits.

All of the foregoing would be quite consistent with Japan's "defense only" doctrine.

Blechman showed unqualified interest in Japan's potentials with respect to nuclear power. Obviously, mention of that potential belonged in the outline. The orientation of what had been said was unexceptionable, except, perhaps, in the implication that Japan should oppose first use of nuclear weapons. I pointed out that I had not advanced that as a recommendation, only suggested that Japan be as ready to consider taking a stand on the issue as are European countries.

WILLIAM WATTS, SCHOOL FOR ADVANCED INTERNATIONAL STUDIES OF JOHNS HOPKINS UNIVERSITY
(December 10, 1982)

William Watts, an associate at the Johns Hopkins School for Advanced International Studies (SAIS), had been the author of many highly regarded publications dealing with public opinion surveys on Japan and East Asia. He was unusually well qualified to observe crosscurrents in American opinions on Japan.

Authorities at the Pentagon, Watts observed, said that the United States and Japan had surmounted significant hurdles in moving towards agreement on central security questions. Currently, the two countries were speaking the same language, and were on track as they focused on respective roles and missions. It was true that Marcos and Soeharto had expressed anxiety about a build-up of Japanese military power, but Secretary Weinberger, during his trip through Southeast Asia, was seen by Pentagon officials to have allayed many of these anxieties. The secretary had, moreover, persuaded the Japanese that the United States would not abandon its interests and involvements in the Pacific region. According to the Pentagon, U.S.-Japanese relations were on a good footing.

At the Department of State, authorities differed, in nuance, among themselves. However, there was agreement that Southeast Asian anxieties about the Japanese military build-up were real and continuing. In talks with the Japanese, Washington pushed too hard. The U.S.-Japanese *agenda* might be agreed, but there was, often, high tension in dealing with specific differences.

Several key figures in Congress felt that Japan could do more to support our mutual interests, and ought to do so: Japan's contribution to defense requirements was insufficient. It should be recognized, however, that doing even much more might not alter conviction that protectionist legislation was proper retaliation against Japan's unfair trade behavior. According to Watts, few members of Congress felt they could dare, these days, to vote against proposals for "reciprocity" or "domestic content." Congressional spokesmen could regret this trend — even try to disassociate themselves from it — but still had to accept it, fatalistically and as a reality of political life. Watts reported that Congressman Clement Zablocki had believed that the Japanese must be told that the danger was very great. Understanding and patience were imperative. There must be no shouting. But success in avoiding mistakes was far from sure.

ADMIRAL NOEL GAYLER,
RETIRED COMMANDER IN CHIEF, PACIFIC FORCES
(December 13, 1982)

Admiral Noel Gayler, author of a widely noted *New York Times Magazine* article on nuclear arms control, a frequent witness before congressional committees, and an astute observer of trends in the Washington foreign policy/security establishment, commented on the outline.

The outline advanced significant and constructive ideas, and drew attention to some important factors largely ignored by Americans.

It was proper to place emphasis on the security implications of Japan's economic role in the area and in the world, and on Japan's successful administration of its own economy. It was surprising that the sensitive security situation of Korea had been dealt with so lightly.

The "defense only" "AWACS concept" was sound and appealing, but should not be oversold. Of foremost importance were Japan's air and navy potentials, structured to conform to "defense only" purpose. Heavy investment in the army was puzzling. Would the army be used to oppose a most unlikely amphibious invasion of Hokkaido? Was it needed for internal security? Was it a vestigial expression of bushido? Would it be used offensively?

Clearly Japan's potentials for surveillance, air defense, and control of sea-lanes/straits were enormous. And, in that connection the "AWACS" capability was highly relevant. Even now, however, E-2C radar coverage went far towards creating the intelligence needed for combat effectiveness. But opportunities for improvement were great. Acoustic, space, and fifth-generation computer technology would profit from Japanese technological sophistication. The case was strong for focus on Japan's "AWACS" potential, with stress on its value in creating efficient CCC (command, control, communications). Currently contemplated ASW (antisubmarine warfare) tactics needed careful review and refinement. Investment in more destroyers, for example, was much less rewarding than investment in submarines, information potentials, detection nets, long-range aircraft, effective antisubmarine weapons, and space.

Gayler saw Soviet surface forces constrained by many factors in the East Asian environment, that would not constrain use of their Backfires or their submarines. These were the serious problems.

Gayler believed the investment in intelligence (and CCC) was often more cost-effective than investment in fighting equipment. Both were needed, of course. But the mix and trade-offs were important. Procurement decisions required precise understanding of overall mission.

On his central preoccupation — nuclear weapons control — Gayler informed me that all members of the Joint Chiefs of Staff (JCS) had favored ratification of Salt II, three had opposed the "dense-pack" basing mode for MX, and that none, he believed, could seriously contemplate actual use of nuclear weapons in combat.

Gayler approved, in general principle, full and unquestioning technology exchanges between the Japanese and American military, but favored case-by-case decisions, owing to the great sensitivity of some U.S. intelligence technology and the serious risk that sharing it with anyone might result in its reaching the Russians.

HOBART ROWEN, *WASHINGTON POST*
(December 13, 1982)

Hobart Rowen, principal economic reporter for the *Washington Post,* and a careful analyst of the Japanese economy, disclaimed authority to comment on the military elements in Japan's concept of comprehensive security. However, on the question of the defense build-up, there was some change in the focus of public interest. A little less was being said about percentages of GNP and more about the previously neglected questions of how Japan might be using its military build-up, and its acquisition of American technology, to get a jump on American business in hitherto weak sectors like Japanese aircraft production. Coproduction of the F-15 might, for example, have presented Japan with opportunity to take off in a field where Boeing had been preeminent.

There were other ramifications of the technology question. Nissan, for example, would be producing trucks in Tennessee, bringing in Kawasaki robots to help do the job. Kawasaki robots were made under license from UNIMATION in Massachusetts. Nissan could easily have used the American instead of the Japanese robot. For Nissan to "buy Japanese" in the United States exacerbated suspicions of Japanese greed.

Rowen had just interviewed Senator Dole, who forecast that the next Congress would be giving even higher priority to dealing with the sensitivities of trade issues than to the sensitivities of Social Security. A "domestic content" bill had passed the House. The Senate would probably hold it up so that technically it would die when the autumn session adjourned. However, during 1983, in some form, it would reemerge in the House and make its way to the Senate.

RICHARD BARNET, AUTHOR
(December 15, 1982)

Richard Barnet, author of *Real Security,* and now working with the *New Yorker* on publication of a just-completed work on the occupation of Germany and Japan, had shown great interest in Japan's concept of comprehensive security. He was particularly interested in understanding what lay behind differences between Washington and Tokyo assessments of "threat."

"Antagonistic collaboration" seemed to be the Japanese estimate of the necessary relationship with the U.S.S.R. And it was a far more rational estimate than the American view that offered three unthinkable options: war, Soviet capitulation, or U.S. capitulation.

What deserved asking was whether responsible leadership anywhere could rationally accept these as being real options — except in a vocabulary intended only for domestic political discourse. What were the real issues between Moscow and Washington? Territorial boundaries? Unpaid debts? In detail, they were trivial. The real problem was ideological, against domestic but also global backdrops. And that problem could not be solved by "enemies." The Japanese seemed to have made that judgment.

Barnet said that he seriously questioned that Moscow had always been committed to fulfilling a preconceived imperial design/intention. He believed, rather, that Russia had always been obsessed with recognition of the costs and risks of losing wars. Roots of Russian paranoia went back to the Mongols, to Napoleon, and, of course, to Nazi Germany.

For Washington to have settled on a fix that the Soviet Union was its "enemy" could be, Barnet feared, suicidal. When we monopolized nuclear weapons, we attributed to the Russians a numerical superiority in conventional forces that would fan out over all of Europe. When Russia acquired nuclear weapons, we pursued a race with Moscow for superiority in all ways. Always, they were the "enemy." Neither side had ever doubted the human carnage that actual use of nuclear weapons would cause. Long ago, about seven years after Moscow had nuclear weapons, it was Washington's assessment that a nuclear exchange would leave 65% of the population casualties. It had not been Russia's "imperial design" that fed the nuclear arms race. In both Russia and the United States, bureaucracies and technologies sustained the momentum, with Russia aiming to gain equality, and the United States aiming to deny it.

Russian behavior had often been stumbling, giving plausibility to the contention that the Russians were, in fact, "barbarians." Many Americans of great wisdom embraced, at one time or another, that conviction — including George Kennan, Averill Harriman, Dean Acheson, and others. Only diffidently did anyone accept the possibility that the Russians might have legitimate anxieties and expectations with regard to their own security, and could be expected to behave with some prudence. It was an irony of history that Nixon and Kissinger achieved success in ending "ideological" confrontation with the Soviet Union, and in placing U.S.$-Soviet relations on the footing of "antagonistic collaboration" characterized in Japanese strategy.

Barnet feared that Japan could do nothing to stop charges of "free ride" without significant structural improvement in the world economy. For Japan to engage in heavy rearmament would, however, not help much. What needed to be understood was that real differences in the U.S. and Japanese situations and capabilities constituted a source of strength and not weakness in the shared strategic environment.

Japan's most effective contribution to security would be for it to do more of what it already does best. The real problems facing Japan and the United States were not, primarily, in military threats presented by the Soviet Union or by North Korea: there were other, more serious threats, which Japan rightly identified. It was to everyone's advantage for Japan to keep a low military profile. A self-defense establishment made up of small and mobile fighting units armed with conventional weapons should suffice. These might be regarded as "high-technology partisans." These partisans, equipped with highly sophisticated, easily transportable weapons, would deny any invading power use of territory.

Modern society had become highly centralized, and thus vulnerable. However, defensive capability was strengthened where large numbers of people, properly armed, could deal with dispersed smaller crises. This was a concept that seemed to underlie Yugoslav defense thinking. Within that concept, there was room for local decision-making and effective maneuver. Engagements that contemplated use of nuclear weapons excluded that possibility: very few made the decision to use the weapon, and victims of their use could be very large in number.

In the United Kingdom, there was the worry that movement towards "high-technology partisans" ran the danger of militarizing society. However, was it clear that an armed populace must necessarily move in that direction? National self-defense planning and tactics must, of course, be geared to particular circumstances: population, terrain, economic assets, mobility, and so forth. Japan's decisions must be guided by Japan's local circumstances. Risks in future wars might arise more from blockade than from invasion. Readiness to deal with that possibility would require other preparations.

In any case, Japan's leverage and relevance to future security threats was far greater in the economic field than through mere possession of weapons. Barnet mentioned in this connection Japanese initiatives designed to ease Third World debt-servicing burdens, to facilitate technology transfers, and to assume greater responsibility for preserving order in the international economic system.

Real resolution of all security fears depended almost entirely on some basic change in the goals and the behavior of the U.S. government and its relationship with the Soviet Union. Anti-Soviet paranoia drove forward the arms race, which drained money and intellectual power away from dealing with the world's real and fundamental problems. Stabilization of arms spending at a much lower level was an essential precondition for peace, and, more important, reform of the American system. The United States needed a new industrial policy, and a change from R and D in which pure science was subsidized by the government with little concern shown for social consequences. Education should be broadened and refined. Greater efficiency should be achieved in use of resources.

If the United States failed to achieve the needed reforms, failure could only lead to increasing divergencies between the United States and Western Europe, and between the United States and Japan. With alliances weakened in this way, other countries would show increasing readiness for accommodation with the U.S.S.R. Western Europe, Japan, and China could all move that way, leaving the United States in relative isolation.

7
SOME CONVERSATIONS IN NEW YORK AND WASHINGTON WITH ASIANS IN INTERNATIONAL ORGANIZATIONS

There were Asians in the international organizations of New York and Washington who were often more perceptive about their own countries from a distance than they were when at home. They could also offer perceptive opinions about American foreign policy trends. I talked to several of them about the outline, knowing that Japan had been among their principal professional preoccupations.

INTERNATIONAL MONETARY FUND (December 3, 1982)

I formed many intimate working associations with the staff of the International Monetary Fund during a time when I was chief U.S. negotiator with Bank/Fund representatives working on rescheduling of the Indonesian debt. This official collaboration began in the mid-1960s. There followed a continuing relationship when, as director of the Washington Center of the Asia Society, I turned to these friends while making preparations for "Williamsburg Meetings" that took place between 1971 and 1981. Thus I became quite well acquainted with the expertise and the private speculative thinking of a rather large and important community of Asian economists resident in Washington. None wished to have the views they held attributed to them personally.

Nevertheless, out of an extended series of conversations with these particularly well-informed and attentive observers of developments in the Pacific region came some very suggestive observations.

All attached importance to the differences of perspective on the Pacific region as a whole when viewed from Washington, from Tokyo, and from Southeast Asian capitals. Differences were often quite radical.

There were very important questions about Japan that were seldom discussed. Why had Japan been merely a follower in strategic questions while being an aggressive, innovative, boldly vigorous competitor otherwise? Was it because the "United States was there"? Was it because, internally, consensus was precondition for action, and Japanese consensus building was prolonged and tortuous? Japan could never have fought World War II by consensus: military authorities at that time controlled decision making. Japan's true capabilities could never be realized without much better appreciation of Japan's motivations. What motivated Japan? Profit was a real and acceptable motive for Japanese. How might that motive be used for purposes other than Japan's present narrow ones?

Japan showed no inclination to go it alone. Japan must always share responsibility with others. Almost everyone recognized the importance, for the good of the world community, of cutting down American charges against Japan of "free ride."

No one believed that there was any easy way that Japan could help to improve matters for the international monetary system acting alone. Japan spent $7 billion in trying to intervene so as to strengthen the yen, but to no effect. An effort by Tokyo to limit capital movements abroad would be undesirable. To raise interest rates might slow flight of yen into dollars, but it would also slow business revival and growth in Japan, and thus reduce trade activity. Deficit financing of spending in Japan would make more sense under present circumstances.

A stronger yen would help other countries. But there was no way to quantify that help, if and when it came. Japan should continue to increase its ODA. Desirable as it would be, a stronger yen should not be seen as a substitute for more ODA.

Expanded technology transfers would help. This could be done by much more foreign investment, not only to the "South," but also to places like the United Kingdom. Foreigners could come to Japan to learn—to the United Nations University, for example. Japan's scientific and engineering literature could be translated into English.

Investment in Less Developed Countries' (LDC) oil potentials would be a sound form of North-South aid. Japan could do this by offering government subsidies to private Japanese concerns looking for business in LDCs. MITI now lent such support to Japanese industry at home. It should extend such help for foreign operations. Also, Japan's successes in energy conservation should be shared with other countries.

Singapore had raised wages twice in two years, trying to move labor-intensive industry elsewhere. Singapore's commitment to "high-tech" enterprise could be helped along by Japanese direct investment. Not much had been invested there, despite efforts by Lee Kwan Yew and Goh Keng Swee to proclaim the virtues of the Japanese model. Japan did more in Malaysia, but prospects there were dimmed by Muslim distrust of the Chinese, who were feared as likely to profit inordinately from absorbing or emulating Japanese management/technology.

Those who had read my outline were startled to see that I had said that the United States viewed Russia as an "enemy." They did not believe that that had been true during détente. Such hostility was not, generally speaking, the feeling of many countries in East Asia, which were more relaxed about the Soviet Union than about China or Vietnam.

Throughout the region, conspicuously large U.S. military spending was not admired. It created worries, largely because budget deficits, high interest rates, and protectionism were thought to be the price for meeting Reagan's military goals. An American presence was desired, but not in a showing of great military force. All economists, speaking in that capacity, were convinced that a cut in U.S. military spending would improve the economic outlook for everyone.

East Asia remained the most dynamic and prosperous part of the less-developed world. And it was true, as stated in my outline, that Japan remained the key to the region's future economic prospects.

EAST ASIAN REPRESENTATION
AT THE UNITED NATIONS
(December 3, 1982)

In New York and Washington there was a very gifted community of diplomats and academics who, by combining Confucian and Western intellectual powers, produced unusually valuable judgments on their own countries, on Japan, and on the United States.

Here are samples:

Comprehensive security was a good, valid concept, but it risked promising too much, and, in its vagueness, excusing inaction on specifics. Inasmuch as Japan lacked talent for conceptualization of something like "its position in the world," for Japanese to have developed a concept like comprehensive security was a good effort.

Japan's commitment to "defense only" was reassuring, and correct. One difficulty of Suzuki's 1000 nautical mile surveillance scheme was that Washington seemed unable to clarify even broadly what it really wanted from Japan militarily. Until that was done, Marcos and Soeharto would worry, and perhaps with some justification.

Actually, Japan had done extremely well for itself and the region — and a good thing, too. Imagine the consequences if Japan had failed, and had continued, after the war, to be an economic cripple as forecast by an authority as eminent as former Ambassador Reischauer. Trade liberalization had been largely achieved, and even to dismantle all remaining restrictions would not solve a continuing problem of trade imbalance.

Chie Nakane might have given clues to understanding a cultural element that caused Japan's difficulties both in Southeast Asia and in the United

States. Japan's cultural habits were hierarchical. This was seen in homes, in schools, in bureaucracies, and in relationships within Japan and abroad. Even foreign countries were assigned to "classes." Conscious of this, Southeast Asians saw Japan as distant and arrogant, and even if Japan did good things, its style often produced negative impressions. When Japan showed active concern with North-South issues, what Japan did came across as showing Japan associated with the North, not with the South. This being so, it was hard for Japan to win whatever it did.

East Asian dissatisfaction with Japan did not produce the side effect of elevating trust or affection for Americans. The present condition of the American economy terrified East Asia. Malignant budget deficits were widely attributed to Washington's extravagant investment in weapons.

Actually, in Korea, specifically, various reactions to U.S. defense spending required differentiation. Military authorities and the general public welcomed American resolution in standing up to the communists. Economists, on the other hand, saw no real security unless there was a radical reduction in interest rates, which they did not consider possible so long as there were large, and even rising, U.S. budget deficits for years to come.

ALI ALATAS, INDONESIAN AMBASSADOR
(December 2, 1982)

Ali Alatas was Indonesia's ambassador to the United Nations, having come to that assignment from being executive secretary to Vice President Adam Malik, and previously being Indonesia's ambassador to the United Nations in Geneva. He had read the outline and welcomed the opportunity to talk about it.

Alatas agreed completely that the ASEAN saw no single outside power as the "enemy." It was the fluctuating and mutually interacting relationship — the waxing and waning influence of the four great powers: China, Japan, the U.S.S.R., and the United States — that potentially constituted the "threat from the North," not individual countries as such. Nixon's alteration of the relationship between the United States and China in the 1970s, and the intense concurrent and subsequent antagonism between the U.S.S.R. and China illustrated such fluctuation.

Alatas considered as pejoratively opportunistic the language of the outline suggesting that "partners in the ASEAN . . . prefer to accommodate to or to wait out troublesome — even alarming — diversities and tensions among friends and adversaries rather than to embrace any outside prescription for achieving some overriding common purpose." ASEAN did not, it was true, want to embrace any outside prescription, but did have its own blueprint for the region — a Zone of Peace, Freedom, and Neutrality.

Alatas said that the Japanese used the term "comprehensive security" rather loosely, without filling in detail or actual intention. Japanese leaders compounded the problem by the vagueness and sometimes mutually contradictory nature of their public statements. Nakasone, for example, was quoted in the *New York Times* as agreeing with Washington that countries should be responsible for their own defense, but as going on to say that Japan should change its Constitution. This kind of contradictory comment created confusion in the minds of many in Southeast Asia.

Alatas was sure that Japan's support of Article 9 in its Constitution contributed to stability in the region: statements like Nakasone's generated doubts — and uneasiness — about the permanence of Japan's "no war" Constitution. Japan must define "comprehensive security" more clearly, or other countries would discount it as a serious expression of Japan's real intention.

Japan could forestall charges of "free ride" without alarming its neighbors in two spheres: military and economic. Japan should improve the *quality* of its self-defense establishment, but not its size. Japan could pay the costs of U.S. troops stationed in Japan. Such a move would not worry Japan's neighbors. Defense of the islands, pure and simple, should be stressed. However, Japanese protection of sea-lanes out to 1000 nautical miles went beyond that mission and might create misunderstanding and cause alarm to Southeast Asians. Japanese defense spending should not, of course, reduce Japan's foreign aid.

In the economic sphere, although Japan was already doing a lot, it could do much more in helping to improve North-South relationships; Japan should pick up the slack. Increasing its contributions for foreign aid would have the double benefit of reducing hostility to Japan and increasing Japan's own security. Specific programs might include special technical assistance, technology transfers, and more generous financial flows for ODA and investment. In the past, Japan had been cautious, holding on to assets until they were no longer needed. By doing much more to share its "know-how" in technology and management, Japan itself could be the gainer.

Alatas found "knowledge as deterrence" completely convincing. By using its knowledge industries, advanced communications, and so on, Japan could greatly increase its defense capabilities. Japan might already be making great strides in this direction: some news reports had hinted that Japan might already be thinking of developing a laser antiballistic missile (ABM) system that was two to three times as effective as the present ABM systems used by the United States and the U.S.S.R. These could, according to Alatas, fundamentally alter the balance in the four-power configuration in the western Pacific.

Alatas considered the idea of an ASEAN Coast Guard quite interesting. Such a nonmilitary coast guard could patrol ASEAN sea-lanes for purposes of enhancing safety at sea, preventing smuggling, and engaging in other similar functions, from which Japan, too, would profit. Japan could materially assist in the funding of such a coast guard without wanting to be in any way involved itself. Alatas wondered why no one in Southeast Asia had yet seized upon the "coast guard" idea. Such an apparatus would be compatible with the ASEAN Zone of Peace, and might be preparation for greater ASEAN independence from the great powers.

8
SOME CONVERSATIONS
AT PEARL HARBOR

On January 5, 1983, I flew to Honolulu for conversations at the Headquarters of United States Forces in the Pacific (CINCPAC).

CINCPAC's responsibilities were very broad, involving over fifty countries in the Pacific and Indian Ocean regions. Japan was, of course, a centerpiece of CINCPAC's strategic planning. My purpose in talking with our commander in chief, Admiral Robert Lyman John Long, and members of his staff was to get comment on Japan's concept of comprehensive security. All had read my outline. All had important observations to offer. Foremost, perhaps, was that congressional anxieties about the condition of the American economy had become, directly and indirectly, a cause of concern for American and Japanese military negotiators — unrelated to strictly military matters.

ADMIRAL ROBERT LYMAN JOHN LONG,
COMMANDER IN CHIEF, PACIFIC FORCES
(January 6, 1983)

Robert Lyman John Long (62) graduated from the Naval Academy in 1943. Following World War II service, he commanded two nuclear submarines, commanded the Atlantic Fleet submarine force, served as vice-chief of Naval Operations and became, in 1979, commander in chief of U.S. Pacific Forces. His scheduled retirement in 1982 was postponed for a year — an unusual action for a flag officer, not done since 1942.

Admiral Long said there would be fewer problems in the U.S.-Japanese security relationship if there were not serious strains in the economic relationship. 1983 was likely to present both countries troublesome economic difficulties and both countries should try to guard against handling those difficulties in ways that could injure the common interests which underlay the basically sound U.S.-Japanese alliance.

Use of any nucelar weapons would, of course, cause great devastation, but in a calculation of effective nuclear deterrence, the mere perception of inferior U.S. capability could be as critical as the numbers and characteristics of the weapons themselves in the free world's dealings with the Soviet Union.

The U.S. submarine part of the Triad guaranteed a second strike "until the day when the seas became transparent." Long knew of no technical or operational breakthrough that would make this possible for the foreseeable future. Nevertheless, Long favored further exploration of a practical mode for land basing of strategic missiles — preferably a mobile basing mode.

Long said that as a former commander of U.S. submarine forces, he might be suspected of a bias in favor of submarine-launched nuclear missiles. He noted that some senior-level navy officials have not strongly supported the navy's strategic nuclear forces because in their opinion it drained money away from what the navy believed it was "supposed to have," in other conventional forces.

On the general subject of nuclear weapons systems, I told Admiral Long that Mao Zedong was reported to have said to André Malraux in 1965:

• Nuclear weapons could not win wars

• Their possession had only symbolic value

• Their utility was only in the imagination

• If a country could make their own invulnerable, six were enough.[10]

Long was amused, but did not agree with that assessment of the relevance of such weapons to effective global deterrence.

MAJOR GENERAL JAMES PFAUTZ, CINCPAC: J-2 (INTELLIGENCE) (January 6, 1983)

Major General James Pfautz (senior intelligence officer at CINCPAC) welcomed the unorthodox structure of the outline. He promised to offer written comment later on its various themes. Some of those subsequent comments are included below.

For a start, he observed that 90% of the motivation to take issue with Japan came from the condition of the American economy. The military relationship was excellent. Unemployment in some of our key industries was stimulating anti-Japanese feelings. Once aroused, other elements entered into deplorable resentment (e.g., some Americans felt that the Japanese gave no evidence of the gratitude they should feel for past American help to Japan, and there was aloofness and insensitivity in many U.S.-Japanese personal relations). A Japanese friend was a friend forever, but friendship was increasingly hard to come by, even for someone who had been in Japan many times. Pfautz spoke calmly about these matters, and brought them up, he said, because it would be tragic for *government* mishandling of these difficulties to exacerbate deteriorating economic relations.

Pfautz did not favor a great Japanese build-up of investment in tanks, ships, and aircraft. The Japanese *people* really did abhor any prospect of war-fighting and those systems that could be seen as offensive in purpose. Military investment should be in passive systems such as antisubmarine warfare (ASW), air defense, and selected reconnaissance platforms, for example. It would be a perfectly proper goal for Japan to strive to improve its intelligence-gathering capability, and with that capability to help us enhance the security of Northeast Asia.

I asked whether Washington would be inclined to sell to Japan the very best version of AWACS. Pfautz said there would probably be little or no concern that Japan would compromise or transfer AWACS technology to the U.S.S.R. They would not.

Pfautz quoted some Japanese sources as saying that there was little possibility of Japan's "rearmament" unless spending reached 5% of GNP. Below that level, Japan's spending on the military establishment could be seen as "preparatory" (i.e., to create a framework for possible development of a modest war-fighting capability *in defense of Japan*).

There were other themes worth taking up:

• To compare the relative influence of Japan's Ministries of Foreign Affairs, Finance, and the Defense Agency with the U.S. Departments of State, Treasury, and Defense;

• To distinguish "keeping the faith" with Article 9 from a profound desire to avoid war; and

• To develop further how Japanese and Americans viewed Soviet capability and intention differently.

Pfautz explained to me the different capabilities, and take-off bases, of land-based strategic Backfires, and those operated by the Soviet navy. The latter were based on the mainland coast, just north of Vladivostok. They were a formidable threat, very dangerous with their new missiles.

REAR ADMIRAL ROBERT CHEWNING, CINCPAC: J-3 (OPERATIONS) (January 6, 1983)

Rear Admiral Robert Chewning was the senior planning officer at CINC-PAC. He, too, had read the outline.

To my surprise, Chewning chose to comment first on reference in the outline to an ASEAN Coast Guard. He recognized the utility of its weather, rescue, antismuggling, antipiracy, straits patrol, and surveillance, etc., functions. He could foresee it as being also a valuable intelligence-gathering apparatus. However, he could see no agreed sense of threat among those who might create it. Moreover, he could not envisage anyone entering into an agreement with "ASEAN." Actually, the ASEAN partners might get further if left alone, with no Japanese involvement.

CINCPAC discussed plans with no "collectivities" in the region. There was bilateral planning with Japan, with Korea, and with the Philippines. CINCPAC did engage in joint exercises with its ANZUS partners, Australia and New Zealand.

If we sought movement towards collective security arrangements in the region, maybe the Five Power Defense Pact would be a place to start. In it Singapore and Malaysia were joined by Australia, New Zealand, and the United Kingdom. Thailand had shown interest in participating. Indonesia had shown interest in possible joint exercises. The United States, without belonging, could collaborate. Lee Kwan Yew might take a lead.

Philippine and Indonesian anxieties about the military build-up of Japan should be taken seriously.

The United States welcomed Suzuki's pledge to defend sea-lanes out 1000 nautical miles. At present, Japanese capabilities were insufficient. Needed air, surface, and subsurface force structures to protect Japan, the Straits, and airspace over Japan were being jointly assessed by a Sea-lanes Communications Defense Study Group.

Within Japan's "defense only" doctrine, it could not acquire carriers. However, a number of Japanese islands, like Iwo Jima, could begin to serve as "fixed carriers." Potentials of that concept were being explored in an Operations Plan being drawn up by the Japanese Staff Office (JSO).

There was a study afoot dealing with Japanese facilities (seaports, ships, etc.) that might be made available to the United States if it were involved in war outside of the Japanese homeland area. The study got under way in June 1982.

AWACS was an Air Force technology/weapons system. E-2C was Navy. Both served U.S. interest in effective forward defense. A Japan-based AWACS would be useful in dealing with the steadily growing Backfire threat, which (with its 200-mile KITCHEN missile) would be particularly dangerous.

Chewning regarded the most serious deficiencies in Japanese defense planning to be force sustainability, coordination of the services, and lack of clarity in understanding constitutional restraints (e.g., how to declare an emergency).

9
CONVERSATIONS IN TOKYO
WITH SOME ARCHITECTS
OF COMPREHENSIVE SECURITY

With my conversations in Washington and Honolulu fresh in mind, I began my survey of opinion in Tokyo by talking with a few old personal friends, who had knowledge of Japan's concept of comprehensive security, its origins, and its present bearing on policy process in Tokyo. Only one was an author of the comprehensive security document, but all had been architects of the concept.

My first extended conversation was with former Foreign Minister Saburo Okita, principal sponsor—with the Carnegie Endowment and Singapore's Institute for Southeast Asian Studies—of this study of "comprehensive security." Shortly before Okita became foreign minister, Prime Minister Ohira had set up the task force that produced the Inoki Report; the report was completed after the death of Prime Minister Ohira and was submitted to Acting Prime Minister Ito, in whose cabinet Okita remained. My second extended conversation was with former Ambassador to Washington and former Cabinet Minister Nobuhiko Ushiba, whose knowledge of the United States had brought him responsibility for frequent cabinet-level negotiation of recurring difficulties in the Tokyo-Washington relationship. My third was with Masamichi Inoki, president of Japan's Research Institute for Peace and Security, formerly director of the Japanese Defense Academy, and author of the Inoki Report. A fourth was with Kiichi Saeki, chairman of the Nomura Research Institute, writer of authoritative articles on comprehensive security, and an internationally recognized Japanese spokesman on defense and security questions. My fifth talk, with Takashi Mukaibo, acting chairman of Japan's Atomic Energy Commission, was forceful demonstration of how Japan could strive to lead the world in peaceful uses of nuclear energy and remain committed obsessively to its nuclear *weapons* allergy. Before each of these interviews I had sent over copies of the outline.

SABURO OKITA, FORMER FOREIGN MINISTER
(January 15, 1983)

Saburo Okita approved the scope and structuring of my outline. The outline had prompted him to ask, however, where Japan would stop if it began to strengthen its military capability. Could an increasingly intimate Japanese identification in U.S global strategy increase danger that conflict anywhere could escalate rather rapidly to a global dimension?

Okita mentioned that former Japanese Ambassador to the United States Koichiro Asakai had been asking recently whether too great intimacy between Tokyo and Washington might mean that conflict between the United States and the Soviet Union in the Middle East or Western Europe could bring a Soviet attack on Japan. Might not Japan do better following the Swedish model? That model would have an integrity that half-hearted cooperation with Washington would lack. In any case, only half-hearted cooperation would eventually be impossible.

Okita then said that the Japanese Foreign Office Director General for Research and Planning, Hisahiko Okazaki, was understood to hold, in contrast, quite another conviction about Japan's national self-interest. Historically, Japan had profited from alliance with Great Britain; the United States now inherited that Anglo-Saxon role. Therefore, for its own long-term good, Japan should make an unmistakable commitment to stand at the side of the United States on all issues of strategic importance.

Okita observed that Japan's antinuclear and disarmament commitments were supported by the socialists, by the Japanese Democratic Party (JDP), and by the LDP. Former Prime Minister Suzuki had championed them forcefully. Actually, however, Japanese diplomats had not been entirely consistent in dealing with nuclear and disarmament issues. They had reliably voted Washington's position on the nuclear freeze issue, until the last United Nations session when, influenced by Suzuki's dovish inclinations, they abstained.

Most Japanese favored movement towards disarmament, especially of nuclear weapons. They were asking why, when need for reductions in defense spending was universally recognized, Japan should accelerate rearming. Olof Palme had been urging the Japanese to play a leadership role on the disarmament issue, and many members of the LDP and Japanese media wanted to agree.

Nevertheless, if there were contrary changes in Japan's own defense spending intentions, changes would be gradual. Spending would not increase sharply unless a majority of the Japanese people become suddenly alarmed by some extreme emergency. Even in such circumstances, Japan would not surge towards acquisition of nuclear weapons.

Okita believed that there was need for some refinement of our vocabularies, so as to reflect some better understanding of the legitimacy of Moscow's fears, and Moscow's apparent determination to foreclose possibility of a real threat to Russia being mounted by nearby antagonistic neighbors. The term "defensive aggression" might be suggestive, or "defensive expansionism." These terms would not deny the facts of Russian behavior, but they might help to modify interpretation of the motivation of unattractive Soviet activity.

It was hard for Japanese to imagine Russian military adventure in East Asia. Still, actual Soviet behavior could present Japan with the necessity of choosing appropriate response, about which there was no real consensus among Japanese. Many Japanese asked how Japan should construe the Soviet contention that military installations on three of the four Northern Islands, which Japan claimed to be its territory, served no anti-Japanese purpose, only much broader Soviet strategic requirements? Or what reply should be made to Japanese who asked how actual Japanese engagement in military conflict with the Russians could ever be contained?

For Okita, Japan's alliance with the United States was the centerpiece of Tokyo's security planning. This presented some often unacknowledged difficulties. The Reagan administration's fierce insistence on steadily increasing defense spending caused many Japanese to hold back from becoming too closely associated with that commitment to spend. Holding back raised questions about how great could be actual cooperation. Should Tokyo cooperate in supporting the purposes of Secretary Weinberger or show sympathy for the purposes of other leading Americans not now in office but well known to their Japanese counterparts, like McGeorge Bundy and Robert McNamara? Such questions troubled Japanese.

Okita spoke of Japan's potentials for deterring enemy use of conventional weapons. He cited a growing literature on Japan's military technology advances, through use of its engineering, electronic, and computer skills. Japan's air-to-surface missile was believed to be better than the French Exocet. Until now, Japan had profited from American preeminence in military technology. This had been a one-way street because of Japan's policy of forbidding foreign sale of military items. There had not been truly reciprocal exchanges of military technology between Japan and the United States. However, applications of industrial technology transferable to military production were known to interest Washington, and Prime Minister Nakasone was going to recognize the need for reciprocity on the basis of the alliance relationship with the United States, which clearly justified such exceptional treatment.

Okita agreed with the outline in its contention that the Japanese economy had contributed to security in the region. However, he did not know how that contention could be quantified. Japan had been a "locomotive," but how could the security implications of that fact be proven?

NOBUHIKO USHIBA, FORMER CABINET MINISTER
(January 18 and 28, 1983)

Nobuhiko Ushiba was Japan's poised and skillful ambassador in Washington during the textile controversy that followed Okinawa Reversion, and during the period of the so-called "Nixon shocks." He was the role model for a large number of Japan's most accomplished younger diplomats, who admired his knowledge of Japan's pre- and postwar diplomatic history, his fearless candor, his tough realism, and his ability to sort out and assess complicated economic and political crosscurrents in the United States. Many retired Japanese ambassadors become advisers to large corporate entities. Ushiba was — exceptionally — in his retirement an active participant center-stage and backstage in the practice of Japan's high-level international diplomacy.

Ushiba said that the outline had not brought out that many of the problems faced by Washington and Tokyo were exacerbated by the kind of thing that had appeared in that morning's newspaper report on Secretary Weinberger's alleged "Defense Guidance Statement" of March 22, 1982. Allusions to *protracted* nuclear war-making, and to war in space, were simply incredible. For Washington to sanction such terrifying strategies by charging the Russians with doing, or intending to do, everything first did not ease Japan's doubts about Washington's own rationality in dealing with such possibilities.

The Russian weapons capability was formidable and Japan was aware of it. However, Japan was also aware of problems facing a badly managed Soviet economy, unresolved ethnic and social strains, failure in Afghanistan, and the far-reaching and dangerous implications of failing to deal wisely with dissidence in Poland and elsewhere in Eastern Europe. For Russia, war would not ease handling any of these difficulties. Just to talk with Russians lessened dangers. There should always be such dialogue, carried on calmly, quietly, and with restraint.

"Free ride" was a loosely and widely used term. Actually it could apply only to the Tokyo-Washington relationship. For Europeans to ever use the term was absurd.

There were, involved in the Washington-Tokyo dialogue on "free ride," Ushiba said, military questions that required answers. Japan had not clarified constitutionally procedures for declaring and dealing with emergencies. Interservice cooperation was poor. Ammunition stocks were low: engagement could not be sustained for more than several days. These deficiencies were real, manageable, and deserved early attention.

The real problem with "free ride," however, was how Japan should deal with the U.S. Congress. For years, the administration and Congress pressed Japan to join it in identifying China as the great threat to the region. Nixon altered that. The Soviet Union then was called the great threat: in Washington's rhetoric Russians became ten feet high and their powers were exaggerated. Actually, a far greater threat than the U.S.S.R. to Japan—and to the world—was a serious breakdown of the international economic system.

Particularly distressing, just now, was congressional advocacy of various protectionist measures aimed at Japan, which revealed a disregard for international rules and treaty obligations. So, it now seemed that the most immediate threat to Japan was, in fact, the U.S. Congress. But what could Japan do to reform attitudes of the Congress when Congress was blaming Japan for what were often shortcomings in the American system itself?

To talk about a "Swedish model" was nonsense. Neutrality like Sweden's had no place in responsible Japanese thinking. Japan was, and should be, fully committed to its alliance with the United States. There were no problems that could not be resolved by calm and reasonable consultations. Prime Minister Nakasone's visit to Washington had shown that such dialogue was possible between the administrations in Tokyo and Washington. Steady evolution and consolidation of that relationship should not be spoiled by recurrences of self-righteousness or hysteria.

There were some real problems in the U.S.-Japanese relationship, even under the obviously pro-American leadership of Prime Minister Nakasone. Washington and Tokyo were generally agreed on Japan's goals. To meet 1987 targets of the Japanese Defense Plan, however, might require annual 10% increases in defense spending after 1984: such increases might well be necessary even to mute charges of "free ride." But could Japan state positively that it was going to meet target dates? If not, Japan should discuss with the United States other dates. They should also discuss the priority to be accorded, for example, to procurement of equipment and to sustainability of actual combat.

Defense of Japan was only one of the many common interests the two countries shared. The United States needed Japan as a partner, supporter, and collaborator in many fields of activity. There was need to devote serious thought to the really critical elements in a long-term plan (e.g., ten-year) for a U.S.-Japanese relationship. Without such a plan and perspective, our leaders could lose sight of the fundamental nature of our relationship. For such a plan to be realistic on the Japanese side would not require a new security treaty, revision of Japan's Constitution, or change in Japan's three nuclear principles, and the Constitution was quite flexible enough to permit exploration of future "collective" security arrangements.

Ushiba expressed interest in what might be Washington's real attitude towards selling to Japan its best technology. He also wondered why Washington did not itself rely more on very high technology combat potentials— such as missiles instead of big-cost items like nuclear battle fleets.

Ushiba acknowledged that defense spending everywhere impaired healthy functioning of the world economy. Only the United States could, effectively, take the lead towards needed worldwide disarmament.

MASAMICHI INOKI,
RESEARCH INSTITUTE FOR PEACE AND SECURITY
(January 14 and 21, 1983)

Masamichi Inoki was editor of the Report on Comprehensive National Security. Now president of the Research Institute for Peace and Security, and formerly president of Japan's Defense Academy, he was well known as mentor of outstanding students, including Masataka Kosaka, Masashi Nishihara, Toru Yano, and others. My talks with Inoki and his Institute colleagues focused on the outline.

Inoki said, recklessly I thought, that he agreed with every word of the outline. Much more could be said, however, about some of its themes. Japanese military forces were woefully deficient. Much military spending was misguided. Investment in tanks was meaningless except in Hokkaido. Instead Japan should destroy the enemy before it landed. For that mission, the navy was too small. The air force was also too small. But the worst part was that the services were not cooperating.

Former Prime Minister Ohira had been a "realistic pacifist," who favored necessary military build-up. In contrast, Suzuki held utopian/pacifist views which, in Inoki's own words, made Japan's concept of comprehensive security just like a highball without whiskey.

Inoki went on to say that in addition to Suzuki's indecisiveness, the time since Ohira's death had been tragically disappointing in another way. President Reagan was almost universally seen as an alarming warmonger who polarized Japanese opinion on the security issue and exacerbated the difficulty of defense planning between Japan and the Reagan administration. Inoki had told Nakasone, just before his departure for Washington, that unless Japan developed its own doctrines, concepts, and plans, Washington would treat Japan as a troublesome protectorate.

Japanese opinion on "comprehensive security" was divided. One side thought the concept was designed to downgrade, and the other side to encourage, development of Japan's own minimum but effective defense capability. The latter faction well understood both the need for tactical war-fighting capability, and a need to refute "free ride." Japan's investments in the E-2C and in P-3C were sound, but still insufficient. AWACS would enhance Japan's independent surveillance capability. Having it, Japan would enter into more equal partnership with the United States.

Retired Admiral Sakonjo, Retired General Tsukamoto, Defense Academy Professor Watanabe, and Institute Research Analyst Tanaka added comment. Sakonjo said that he agreed with Admiral Long, Admiral Gayler, and General David Jones that there were higher priorities than a build-up of Japanese destroyer forces. The Soviet navy was vulnerable on the high seas of the Pacific Ocean, but well protected in the Sea of Japan and the Sea of

Okhosk. Japan's mission should be to control the Straits, for which large naval vessels were unnecessary. In the Pacific, Soviet submarines were a real threat. The P-3C, armed, was better able to cope with them than were destroyers. Danang and Cam Ranh Bay were naval bases in only a quite limited sense: they would be highly vulnerable in time of war, and useful only in conflict, or imminent conflict, between Third World countries.

Sakonjo reported, parenthetically, that Mitsubishi was making a better air-to-surface missile than the Exocet. Tsukamoto added that the Japanese model was more accurate, had longer range, had all-weather capability, and was cheaper.

Watanabe, of the National Defense Academy, observed that the outline did not mention the United Nations. As brought out in the Inoki Report, the United States-Japan treaty relationship was, of course, important. However, for the Third World, with its advocacies of a "new economic order," the United Nations was important as the forum where Japan could offer them sympathy and support. Japan could easily seem to be contradictory/hypocritical to both the United States and to Third World countries in United Nations discussions.

Watanabe drew attention to the reference to "limited conventional" military engagements. "Skirmishing" might be possible, he said. However, it was unlikely that anything more protracted could remain "limited" for very long. Quite soon any significant "limited conventional" engagement would bring the United States into the action, and create possibilities of nuclear confrontation. Most Japanese believed that nuclear weapons could only deter: they did not want them ever to be used.

Watanabe, Tanaka, Tsukamoto, and Sakonjo speculated about circumstances under which Japan might contemplate acquiring nuclear weapons. Watanabe could imagine no circumstances, except termination of the security treaty. Tanaka acknowledged a Japanese nuclear allergy, but observed some growing indifference and cynicism on this issue among young Japanese. Tsukamoto said that the treaty could be terminated and Japan rearmed, but Japan would still not produce nuclear weapons unless Korea and/or Taiwan possessed them. Sakonjo said that if the treaty ended, Japan might decide that going nuclear would be useless and, instead, seek an accommodation with Moscow, something like Finland's.

KIICHI SAEKI, NOMURA RESEARCH INSTITUTE
(January 21, 1983)

Kiichi Saeki, president of Nomura Research Institute, did not need to review his thoughts on "comprehensive security." His writing and previous conversations with me had already been absorbed into the outline.

Before going to Washington, Nakasone had talked together with Saeki, Ushiba, Okita, Akio Morita, Isamu Yamashita, and Takashi Hosomi. Saeki liked the fact that Nakasone had used the word "alliance" before going, and had told the Japanese what he would tell Americans about beef and citrus fruits, and then had stuck to it.

Saeki discussed Nakasone's *Washington Post* interview. The reference to Japan's being an unsinkable aircraft carrier implied, if examined fairly, Japan's "defense only" mission. The reference to "four straits" was puzzling: the fourth might be in the north, or the Korean side of Tsushima. Nakasone wanted debate on the constitutional revision, but there would be no change while he was prime minister.

Talk with Saeki always shows what are likely to be some of the current preoccupations of the small community of Japanese defense analysts of which he is a highly respected senior member.

Saeki told me that he was about to leave with other representatives of government and academic institutions for a six-day conference in Moscow, organized by the Russian Institute for Oriental Studies. From Japan's standpoint, these meetings were important to support. Saeki had just finished participating in a U.S.-Japanese bilateral conference at Oiso called to work out some agreed recommendations to governments. He had strongly approved, in particular, a recommendation calling for improvement of consultative procedures.

Preparation for a Trilateral Commission meeting in Rome had given him opportunity to reflect on arms control/reduction possibilities. With Andropov holding the reins of power, there might be improved possibilities for compromise. Though there could be negotiating leeway with respect to the Pershing II — which could hit Russia in six minutes — NATO should not give up its slow, second-strike cruise missiles. The Intermediate Nuclear Force (INF) negotiations were critical, inherently and as preparation for the Strategic Arms Reduction Talks (START). Saeki made two further comments: Europe-targeted SS-20s should not be deployed to where they threaten China and Japan. Participants in the preparatory committee for the Rome meeting, Saeki said, opposed renunciation of the "first use" option; they agreed to the necessity of build-up of conventional forces.

Saeki hoped that Secretary Shultz's trip to China would be the occasion for changing President Reagan's provocative overcommitment to the Taiwan Relations Act. Deng Xiaoping's desire to design coexistence schemes for Taiwan and for Hongkong should be respected as genuine, and should be supported. What was interesting was whether Peking's arrangements for Hongkong would be a precedent for Taiwan, or vice versa. No contract with either was likely until someone else had succeeded Chiang Ching-kuo.

Saeki said that, important and interesting as arms talks were, they shrank to irrelevance compared to dangers — profound and far-reaching — now threatening the world economy.

TAKASHI MUKAIBO, ATOMIC ENERGY COMMISSION
(January 26, 1983)

Takashi Mukaibo, a chemist, was formerly the universally admired president of Tokyo University, which some describe, awesomely, as having the standing in Japan of something like Harvard, Yale, and Princeton *combined*. He was now the acting chairman of Japan's Atomic Energy Commission. A politician was always the chairman; the acting chairman was the Commission's effective chief operating executive.

Mukaibo said that the tasks of the Atomic Energy Commission were to promote nonmilitary use of nuclear energy, to assure balanced development of a national program, and to make long-term plans. Japan had made an irreversible commitment to develop the power potentials of nuclear energy. The government was spending $1.2 billion yearly on research and development alone. The private sector was investing three to five times more on construction, and engaging also in its own research. One-sixth of the government's R and D budget for nuclear energy was devoted to fusion in recent years. Although a theoretical breakthrough on fusion might be possible in the 1990s, commercial application was not likely before the twenty-first century.

Mukaibo knew, of course, that the nuclear power industry in the United States was in the doldrums. Japan's situation, however, was, he said, entirely different: Japan could not survive without reliance on nuclear energy. Fluctuation of oil prices would not affect Japan's commitment to its program. Already it produced 20% of Japan's electricity. By 1990, nuclear energy was expected to supply about 30% of Japan's requirement for electricity, which was 11% of total energy consumption. And the commitment to breeder reactor technologies was also firm, motivated as it was by a need to gain independence through use of plutonium from dependence on outside nuclear materials. Starting with technology borrowed from the United States and France, Japan had already begun to make technological improvements. Japan was acutely aware of the dangers of waste disposal, and of preserving plant safety. However, this would not deter it from moving right ahead through light water, to advanced thermal, to breeder reactors, even though the existence of breeder reactors could be seen as increasing threats to the effectiveness of arms control. Knowing this, Japan could only declare that Japan's interests and policies with respect to arms control were simple and clear. Japan accepted the obligations of signatories of the Non-Proliferation Treaty. Japan prohibited by law use of nuclear materials for weapons production. Japan cooperated, without reservation, in the International Atomic Energy Agency

(IAEA). IAEA representatives resided in Japan. Japan accepted IAEA safeguard procedures, had studied their requirements on its own, and had recommended ways to improve them.

Japan was ready to cooperate with other countries in peaceful uses of atomic energy. So far, cooperation had been most active with respect to medical, industrial, and agricultural uses of radioisotopes, and in basic research. Japan cooperated with almost all East Asian countries except Burma and North Korea. Hitherto, the connection with Peking had been modest, and has largely involved exchanges of personnel. There had been Chinese missions discussing greater cooperation. In addition, the Atomic Energy Commission had received requests through governmental or nongovernmental channels from Indonesia, the Philippines, South Korea, and Taiwan for cooperation in getting training for personnel working in nuclear power plants. Peking had asked that their designs for nuclear power plants be reviewed: this was being done outside of Japanese government channels. A privately organized Atomic Industrial Forum provided a setting where Japanese, Chinese, and others could engage in informal consultation. Mukaibo said that none of this activity so far had caused him to be concerned about dangers of misuse anywhere.

Mukaibo considered the adequacy of energy, together with the adequacy of food and military defense capability, to be the critical elements in Japan's concept of comprehensive national security. Stress on nuclear power potentials should be seen in that context.

Mukaibo took no exception to the outline, other than in disagreeing vehemently with its final paragraph (which allowed for the possibility of a Japanese decision to acquire nuclear weapons). Japan's interest in nuclear capability was strictly and absolutely nonmilitary. Even if Japan's treaty with the United States were terminated, and American military forces withdrawn, Japan would not contemplate having nuclear weapons. Japan's commitment never to have nuclear weapons was irreversible. There was, in Japan, no group, Mukaibo said, that thought otherwise.

Nakasone was, Mukaibo believed, a very careful person. As Prime Minister, he had said nothing to raise doubts about his own commitment to eschew nuclear weapons.

Mukaibo admitted that Japan's Atomic Energy Commission had not discussed, as a general proposition, renunciation of first use of nuclear weapons. The issue of first use faced only the nuclear powers. Japan was not involved. Faithful to the three nuclear principles of no possession, no production, and no "transit," Japan would never have such weapons located in Japan.

Mukaibo held the personal view that nuclear weapons should never be used by anyone, anywhere. This, he believed, was the majority opinion in Japan. His own conviction, he said, had been influenced, in part, by participation in a United Nations Advisory Group, set up by U Thant back in 1967, to consider the effects of using nuclear weapons. John Palfrey represented the United States, Solly Zuckerman the United Kingdom. Mukaibo had worked up a presentation of facts on biological consequences, as observed after the bombing of Hiroshima and Nagasaki, and after the United States testing, thereafter. For many years, the world had known the facts. Mukaibo's own conviction was that any use of nuclear weapons would produce an unimaginable world calamity.

10
CONVERSATIONS IN TOKYO WITH SOME JAPANESE FOREIGN SERVICE OFFICERS

A remarkably well-informed, disciplined, poised, and self-assured generation of Japanese foreign service officers was rising to what, in the United States Department of State, would be the assistant secretary/ambassadorial level. They had, during their careers, dealt with economic, political, and military problems. Many had impressive linguistic skills. They seemed to enjoy discussing general ideas important to Japan, and to the world, with a style and flair for stimulating speculation seldom found in Japan before World War II, or just afterwards. Eight or ten of these officers, old friends of mine, were in the Foreign Ministry during my Tokyo stay. All were ready to talk about Japan and Japan's concept of comprehensive security.

HISAHIKO OKAZAKI,
DIRECTOR GENERAL, RESEARCH AND PLANNING
(January 13 and 26, 1983)

Hisahiko Okazaki was director general of the Japanese Foreign Ministry's Bureau for Research and Planning. Among his previous assignments had been Washington, Seoul, and the Defense Agency. During 1982, Okazaki had been a traveling guest scholar at many American centers of defense analysis. He was a gifted and often daring writer.

Okazaki could find no fault in the outline, except in insignificant detail. However, he doubted that after Prime Minister Nakasone's trip to Washington the concept of comprehensive security as talked about by Suzuki would survive the spring of 1983. To a great extent, "comprehensive security" had been a slogan rather than a policy of any real originality—as was the case with almost every declaratory policy of a government in a society of mass politics. "Comprehensive security" was designed to cast a conceptual cloak over already existing elements in Japan's foreign policies. The Inoki Report published in 1980 had really failed to take account of radical changes that had already occurred in Japan's strategic environment, especially since 1975. There was now taking place slowly increasing appreciation of the impact on the world produced by the fall of the Shah and the imposition on the United States of additional burdens for the defense of the Gulf. Concurrently, a build-up of Soviet SS-20s, Backfires, the Soviet army, navy, and air force in the Pacific was taking place at a time when American powers were clearly thinning out in the Indian and Pacific Oceans. Japan's policies now had to change to deal with those new realities. Specifically, Japan had to recognize the necessity of being ready to make appropriate response to emergency situations based on scenario studies.

Okazaki said that only the balance of power should influence Japanese national decision on the defense requirement, not tradition, nor an urge to make peace with the U.S. Congress. Power was crucial.

HIROAKI FUJII, DIRECTOR GENERAL, ASIA
(January 17 and 27, 1983)

Hiroaki Fujii was deputy director general of the Asian Affairs Bureau of the Foreign Ministry, after having held senior positions in several other bureaus and embassies including a brilliant tour as counselor in Japan's Washington Embassy. He was one of a small group—small in any diplomatic service—of diplomat/intellectuals.

Fujii had studied the outline before I talked with him. He had been wondering, it seemed, as had I, about how to quantify (or otherwise clarify) Japan's aid contributions to developing countries, notably to ASEAN. He mentioned trade, official development assistance, private foreign investment, and various economic cooperation undertakings of mutual benefit. Statistics existed for this. In addition, but quite difficult to measure, Japan transferred to ASEAN countries technologies, computer software, counsel on procedures of scientific investigation, and on management methods.

Impossible to measure, but nevertheless real, Japan helped by serving as a model, within which, somehow, people were driven by an ethical compulsion to work.

Hard for the Japanese to talk about, also, was Japan's increasingly effective capacity to render nonmilitary assistance to countries bordering on conflict areas. Egypt, Turkey, Pakistan, and Thailand were examples. At the end of 1979, when the Soviet Union invaded Afghanistan, Japan immediately doubled its aid to Pakistan, and Japan has since been the largest donor of economic and humanitarian aid to Pakistan. Thailand had, for reasons both humanitarian and connected to Kampuchea, received soft loans and grants (ODA) from Japan which totaled Y450 billion on a commitment basis between FY 1978 and FY 1982. And both Pakistan and Thailand had declared their gratitude.

The next phase in Japan's development was to become a technological giant. Real power lay in that field, not in mere economic power or in possession of destroyers. Fujii liked what the outline said about knowledge/technology. Kent Calder and Roy Hofheinz had written in *East Asia Edge* about similar tendencies in other East Asian countries. And, although not about Japan specifically, Marilyn Ferguson's *Aquarian Conspiracy* cast light on the holistic characteristics of Japanese change.

Perhaps a unique quality in Japanese instinct was to shrink things. The bonsai pine was an example. The miniaturization of many industrial technologies was another. "Comprehensive security" must take account of and exploit these essential tendencies in Japan's evolution. For example, Japan said that the United States must learn to accommodate to Japanese competition, but no less Japan must do the same with respect to its rapidly modernizing East Asian neighbors.

Fujii turned to Japan's military defenses. "Sea-lane defense" had been misunderstood by some Asian friends. Both Soeharto and Marcos had declared their alarm because, for them, the term evoked "life line," and "life line" foreshadowed, eventually, Japanese naval activity in their waters and straits. Fujii believed that since there was no intention whatsoever on the part of the Japanese Government to extend its naval patrols to ASEAN waters, ASEAN leaders, in time, would understand Japan's position.

Fujii spoke of Prime Minister Nakasone's late April 1983 tour through the ASEAN capitals, and to Brunei. For that trip it would be desirable if Japan's economic, cultural, and technological contributions to that region could be convincingly quantified. Present data was unsatisfactory. Fujii suggested that I discuss with his staff how to achieve more effective quantification of the facts. Such clarification would be a major objective of Prime Minister Nakasone's trip to ASEAN.

HIROSHI KITAMURA, DIRECTOR GENERAL, NORTH AMERICA
(January 27, 1983)

Hiroshi Kitamura was director of the North American Affairs Bureau of the Foreign Ministry, having served before in various other bureaus and embassies, notably the OECD in Paris and, quite recently, as Consul General in San Francisco. My own acquaintance with him began after he had spent a year at the Bowie/Kissinger Center for International Affairs at Harvard, where he had written a brilliant essay on factors of national psychology that had complicated and often aggravated U.S.-Japanese relations. Kitamura had coordinated preparations for Prime Minister Nakasone's trip to Washington and had accompanied him. We talked together after his return.

I mentioned having heard in Tokyo two views on the Japanese-U.S. relationship: some urged acceptance of Washington's lead on all strategic issues, while others urged greater separateness. Almost everyone considered the Prime Minister's visit to be a threshold event, believing that things never would be quite the same as before. But what would be the new direction if this were to be so?

Kitamura said that Prime Minister Nakasone clearly brought a new style to his office, in other words a conspicuous determination to make decisions that had been needed to resolve problems between Japan and the United States for a long time. Despite press interpretations of what he had been saying about such matters as making Japan "an unsinkable aircraft carrier," "defense of sea-lanes," and "controlling three straits around Japan when attacked," all of these concepts still fell within the framework of Japan's defense policies accepted and practiced in previous cabinets. How expressed might be different, but the substance of the concepts was all the same. The underlying idea was that Japanese should make their own efforts to defend their own country, but Japan could not do it alone and, therefore, it needed assistance from the United States under the security pact with the United States.

Out of the Washington conversations came evidence that Japan should and would take needed initiatives, and not merely react to pressures from Washington.

U.S.-Japanese relations had not entered a new era, but the visit had helped to surmount a stalemate and changed the atmosphere between the two countries. Washington appreciated the work Nakasone had done during the fifty days he had been in office in resolving many difficult problems in both economic and defense fields. Japan's image had been improved. Answers were given to charges that Japan managed its foreign trade unfairly. Both sides recognized the need for realistic and cool-headed consultation. This, alone, was an important achievement, against a background of American talk that had often been emotional, unreal, and anything but cool some months ago.

Kitamura recognized in view of the present severe international situation the need for Japan to reinforce its defense capabilities in various fields — stocks of ammunition and spare parts were low, and vulnerability of equipment should be greatly reduced. Japan should build up its defenses, but not merely to gain good will from the U.S. Congress or U.S. military services. Kitamura firmly believed that Japan should, on its own initiative, continue its defense efforts in accordance with its Constitution and basic defense policy, which should serve the genuine interest of the Japanese people and of the U.S.-Japanese partnership.

MIZUO KURODA, AMBASSADOR, UNITED NATIONS
(January 31, 1983)

Late in January 1983, Mizuo Kuroda was Japan's ambassador designate to the United Nations, soon bound for New York. I had known him well, years back, when he was minister of the embassy in Washington and had seen him in Tokyo, infrequently but always with instant recovery of readiness to talk. Following his highly successful tour of duty in Washington, Kuroda undertook various responsibilities in several bureaus in the Foreign Ministry before going on to be Japan's ambassador to Yugoslavia, Egypt, and Australia. Always well informed, Kuroda was, this time, briefly a bystander reflecting, with detachment, on the situation in Japan, following the prime minister's visit to Washington. We had agreed to talk about "comprehensive security."

Kuroda said that the Japanese people had little feeling of extended threat to Japan's security. What feeling there was lay at the fringe of their consciousness. Meanwhile, recollection of the military disaster of World War II was sharp. There was, consequently, not much popular support for the military establishment.

Japan's geographic situation had been a strategic asset for over a thousand years. It was true, of course, that Russia was nearby, but Siberian East Asia was a sort of a tail of the Russian "bear," whose paws reached westward from European Russia. Moreover, even in the Far East, Russia's main concern was China.

Considering Japan's assessment of the risk of military threat, the present level and structure of its forces were, probably, about right. Adjustment within that structure would be desirable. There should be, as certain experts advocated, greater reliance on defensive surface-to-air missiles, and less reliance on expensive aircraft with their vulnerable radar sites. Defensive missiles were cheaper and probably less vulnerable than aircraft.

When Washington talked to Tokyo about defense matters it was always as a global power. Japan spoke only about its local/regional responsibilities. Australia was like Japan in one respect: both were primarily concerned with their local defense needs, rather than with Washington's global strategies. The NATO alliance was more reciprocal, but even in Europe real concerns were local, unlike Washington's conception of global responsibility.

Japan's commitment to protect sea-lanes, if interpreted fairly broadly, might worry the ASEAN countries. Australia would also object were the commitment to be interpreted to involve entry of the Japanese navy into Australia's backyard. These points should be taken into consideration in future clarification of Japan's "sea-lanes" mission.

Few Japanese can imagine "protracted war." When four years(!) of warmaking are mentioned the Japanese mind cannot comprehend the possibility.

Kuroda observed that "comprehensive security" embraced other than military elements. There should be more ODA, although Japanese, feeling the pinch of budgetary restraint, were concerned that such aid does not always bring about expected results or help those poor people who most needed it. Technology transfers were desirable and should also be facilitated, but ready absorption of technology was often impeded by deficiencies in the education or motivation among those to whom it was offered. Cultural exchanges were highly desirable, but their value should not be exaggerated. Great Britain had made a profound cultural impact on the world, but that achievement represented a hundred years of persistent effort. Japan should not, perhaps, be too discouraged by the limited potential of its nonmilitary contributions to security. Looking at the East Asian region, countries there seemed to be doing better than countries in Africa, the Middle East, and Latin America. Although such an achievement was chiefly the result of indigenous efforts and assets, it might be said that the relationship with Japan had also played a role.

11
CONVERSATIONS IN TOKYO WITH SOME JAPANESE WORKING OUTSIDE GOVERNMENT

Open and forthright as they were, Japanese government servants measured their words. In some indefinable and not unattractive way they were detached analytically, but fundamentally they defended Japanese policies. There had flourished in Japan, however, a community of highly sophisticated analysts of Japanese and world affairs who suffered no such inhibition: often, they were ready to criticize, even condemn, Japanese policy. They were independent-minded university professors, journalists and editors, and re- tired government servants who spoke their minds boldly. Many wrote cons- tantly, as scholars or as journalists. Their opinions were, often, so well organized that it seemed that from memory they were "quoting themselves." All had views on "comprehensive security." To talk with them was highly rewarding.

YASUO TAKEYAMA, *NIHON KEIZAI SHIMBUN*
(January 19, 1983)

Yasuo Takeyama was the managing director/editor of *Nihon Keizai,* a newspaper which in Japan has the quality and business orientation of the *Wall Street Journal* in the United States. A prolific writer, Takeyama has won, as well, attention and respect as a brisk and provocative ad lib par- ticipant in conferences held in the United States, Europe, and Asia. Although personally wounded by the atomic bombing at Hiroshima, Takeyama showed no evidence of nuclear allergy or tendency towards pacifism. Uncharacteris- tic for a Japanese, Takeyama's conversational style was often didactic, and laced with comic exaggeration. Americans to whom he refers on a first name basis would awe most Georgetown "insiders."

"Comprehensive security" was, Takeyama flatly stated, an alibi for doing little in fostering rapid defense build-up. Talk about Japan's closing the straits was just that: talk. Japan could not do it without its own nuclear weapons capability.

U.S. global military strategies were very obscure. For invulnerable second-strike capability, would it depend eventually on Trident or the MX? He hoped it would be the Trident. Obscurity about strategy was a cloak, Takeyama suspected, for recklessly seeking extravagant redundancies of combat capability and tolerating intense rivalry among the U.S. military services scrambling for money.

AWACS had some appeal, but it was an old-fashioned concept. A Japanese satellite would be better. *Nihon Keizai* had urged investment in satellite intelligence-gathering technology five years ago.

The U.S.-Japanese entente needed, critically, a new definition of common purpose. Pacific Asia was the key to the future of the world. When Europe became "Finlandized," the center of gravity for the world would shift to the Pacific region (even excluding the People's Republic of China). Washington and Tokyo should prepare, now, for that event.

Japan had good cause for calling the Soviet Union a potential adversary as long as Russian forces illegally occupied the Northern Islands.

Takeyama admitted holding unorthodox views on Japan's defense establishment. That establishment should be under the command of a United Nations Headquarters located in Japan or a Western Alliance Command. It should be separated from the context of the U.S.-Japanese security pact. Japan's homeland defense capability should be largely based on missiles and sophisticated interceptors. And Japanese purchases of disgustingly "obsolete" American equipment should cease. "Comprehensive security" should be as overall and as precise as Switzerland's "concept of general defense," which was adopted as national policy by the Swiss in July 1973.

SEIZABURO SATO, TOKYO UNIVERSITY
(January 18, 1983)

Seizaburo Sato was a member of the faculty of Tokyo University, a frequent contributor of articles to the Japanese press, and a leading member of a multi-university intellectual organization—the Forum for Policy Innovation—lobbying for reform of Japanese foreign policy. He was, three years previously, a member of the Inoki Task Force. We discussed the outline.

Sato reminded me that the report was already out of date, in two respects. First, the world economy was much more fragile than had been foreseen. Without a stable world economy there could be no security, for Japan or anyone else. Second, the Soviet Union was confronting many acute difficulties not foreseen three years ago. This necessitated reevaluation of the Russian threat.

These changes in the realities of the world situation required redefinition of policy priorities. The world's economic system must be reformed and strengthened. Japan, for example, must completely liberalize agriculture and services. Imports of beef and citrus fruits must be freely permitted: Japan should accept that political difficulty, while at the same time administering a system that would solve over five or ten years the economic problems of Japanese agricultural producers. Japan must be prepared to accept some American and European protectionism without undertaking protectionist retaliation of its own.

As to the Soviet Union, the outlook for Moscow was far more troubling than three years ago. Economic and ethnic problems were acute. The Afghan venture was a costly failure. Sino-Soviet rapprochement, if taking place at all, would be slow. Vietnam was fretful, if not actually hostile, much of the time. Russia's spending on its military establishment was enormous, but its technology lagged behind the West. If the United States, its NATO allies, and Japan could devise improved procedures for cooperation, their technological advantage over the Russians would increase. The time was right for exploring arms control/reduction possibilities.

Japan's new Forum for Policy Innovation, headed by Yasusuke Murakami and Chikashi Moriguchi of Tokyo and Kyoto Universities, was made up of a nationwide representation of academic and business leaders. Sato was a leading spirit in guiding its deliberations and gave me a copy of its manifesto to study. The Forum had recommended specific goals. The Forum had urged spending 3% of GNP for "comprehensive security" purposes in ten years. ODA should rise from 0.34% to 1% of Japan's GNP and become about 40% of total contributions recorded by the Development Assistance Committee (DAC). Contributions to high-technology improvement of food and energy potentials, and to creation of reserves, should absorb another 1% of GNP. Military spending should be held at 1%.

KAZUHITO ISHIMARU, *MAINICHI*
(January 19, 1983)

Kazuhito Ishimaru was a senior editor at *Mainichi,* a newspaper often compared to the *Washington Post*. Formerly he was *Mainichi's* bureau chief in Washington. No less aware than Takeyama of crosscurrents of Japanese and American intention and opinion, Ishimaru was more introspective and analytical.

Although it had been our intention to talk about "comprehensive security," Ishimaru talked largely about personalities within the LDP, and how their opinions, as viewed by the media and public, might have a bearing on Japan's security policies.

Nakasone had played his cards during the fall of 1982 with great skill. Unless he had bad luck, he would remain Prime Minister for four years. His leading eventual competitor within the LDP would likely be Kiichi Miyazawa who was inheriting leadership of the Ohira/Suzuki faction.

The Nakasone/Miyazawa interpretations of LDP policies and priorities were often compared. Both were fully committed to alliance with the United States, with Miyazawa more inclined than Nakasone to resist pressure from Washington to move beyond creating minimum self-defense forces. Miyazawa had known the Japanese economic situation well; for many years he held the Planning, MITI, and Foreign Ministry portfolios in LDP cabinets. Nakasone could claim little or no personal authority on economic matters. Miyazawa favored opening the Japan market, increasing internal demand, and extending more foreign aid: these were not issues on which Nakasone was known to have independent views.

Ishimaru said that Japan was, just now, interested in the apparent easing of some Sino-Soviet tensions: the Foreign Ministry was believed to be worried. Nakasone was said to favor doing what was possible to create roadblocks in the easing of those relations. Miyazawa, on the other hand, was said to approve some reduction of Peking-Moscow tensions. In the event of some real movement by Peking towards Moscow, Nakasone would advocate higher levels of defense spending. Miyazawa would recommend making appropriately friendly approaches to both Peking and Moscow.

Ishimaru said that Nakasone's detractors complained that he was too militaristic, and Miyazawa's detractors said he was too intelligent.

KENICHI ITO, AUTHOR (January 17, 1983)

Kenichi Ito was a professor of international politics, a writer, and a colleague in various joint undertakings involving Japanese and American academic personalities. A promising young foreign service officer, he was on the personal staff of Japan's ambassador to Washington in 1973-1975. He negotiated with North Vietnamese, as director of the Southeast Asian Division in Tokyo's Foreign Office, on Japan's normalization of relations with Hanoi in 1975-1976. He also served in Moscow in 1963-1965 and could speak Russian fluently. We discussed themes of my outline.

Ito said that he had written a book on the meaning of the Soviet threat to Japan. The foreign policy of Russia, both Imperial and Soviet, had always followed, he said, two basic principles. One was an uninterrupted pursuit of territorial expansion. Another was a tendency, with historical and cultural roots, to stand back from confronting any stronger opponent. In Japan only the first principle was debated. Those who denied it advocate the policy of unarmed neutrality, and those who overestimated it alarm the nation by referring to "an impending threat of Soviet invasion of Hokkaido."

The second principle was almost completely ignored by the public. However, only by taking adequate cognizance of the second could Japan develop a balanced strategy for its own security. More precisely, Ito contended, the Russians would never dare invade Japan if the United States maintained its strategic equivalence, if not superiority, vis à vis the Soviet Union. However, if the U.S.-Japanese alliance collapsed, if Japan were only lightly armed, if disunity arose from an erosion of national will within Japan, if Japan's diplomatic approaches towards the Soviet Union failed, and if Sino-Japanese friendship cooled, Russia's temptation to attack Japan would grow. In the absence of a U.S.-Japanese alliance, Ito went on to say, Japan would have to consider having its own Trident II-type nuclear ballistic missile submarine (SSBN) hiding in the Pacific as its strategic deterrence. Such security would involve astronomical costs and would isolate Japan from its neighbors, much as happened in the 1930s.

TORU YANO, KYOTO UNIVERSITY (January 23, 1983)

Toru Yano was a professor at Kyoto University. Born in China, he was a remarkable linguist, precise in English, and fluent in German, Thai, Burmese, and Indonesian. He had been a frequent traveler to Southeast Asia, and a writer whose articles appeared in both popular and scholarly journals.

We met in Kyoto to talk about the outline.

Yano observed that many themes treated in the Inoki Report predated the report, but the concept, as such, was Ohira's. Acceptance of the concept never gained national consensus. The late Takuya Kubo, of Japan's Defense Agency, strongly supported it, but Kaibara, an avowed LDP "hawk," did his best to discredit it.

Few Japanese argued, as I had, that the mere functioning of the Japanese economy contributed to security in the Pacific region. Japanese were inclined to refer to their economy only as being the "growth pivot."

The outline correctly described Japan's sense of a Russian threat, but the outline should have gone on to mention Japan's desire to explore constructive relationships with the Russians. Nagano, of Nippon Steel, was going to Moscow, almost immediately after Nakasone's return from Washington. Ishida, a pro-Soviet LDP Diet member, spoke constantly of promising potentials for collaboration with the Soviet Union. There were frequent, extensive, and productive Japanese-Soviet talks outside of government channels, for example at the Japan-Soviet Roundtable, which Shigeo Nagano, Munenori Akagi, Hirohide Ishida, Shigeyoshi Matsumai, and various LDP members attended. Prestigious nongovernment personalities like Inoki, Saeki, Masataka Kosaka, and Yano himself also met at sessions of the Peaceful Asia Conference with Georgi Arbatov, Yevgeniy Primakov, Nikolay Inozemtsev, and others. A business-oriented newspaper like *Sankei* could be sternly anti-Soviet, and still play up the desire of Japan's business leaders to establish Soviet connections.

The Japanese right wing, Yano went on, harped on the possibility of Russian attack. Except for some in the Japanese Defense Agency, few others did so. And this, of course, raised an interesting question. If there were no credible threat, Yano argued, there could be no "free ride." Many asked how Japan would react to departure of United States forces from the region. Even then, Yano believed, the Russians would not attack. The possibility could not, of course, be totally excluded, but Michio Morishima, a Japanese economist in London, had written an article for *Bungei Shunju* arguing that if most improbably Japan were to be subjected to attack, it should surrender unconditionally: war against the Russians could never yield any conceivable profit for Japan. Morishima's argument was that any war-making — not just nuclear war-making — was, in Japan's calculus, an unmitigated calamity.

Yano said that Japan's attitudes towards China and towards Russia were totally different. Japanese never lumped the two countries together. For Japanese, China would always be seen as the home of the greatest cultural inheritance of all history: over centuries, Japan's debt to China had been incalculable. For Japanese, Russia was just a "bear," to which Japan owed nothing.

Yano had agreed completely with the outline's contention that "knowledge is power," and was only surprised that the Japanese themselves had not been discussing that concept that way themselves. The progression to "knowledge as deterrence" prompted him to speculate on implications. He had been intrigued by a concept developed by Yonosuke Nagai, now at Harvard, that power was "potentiality." For greatest effect, discrete "potentials" should not be "assembled." Thus, actual power might be diminished by producing weapons as compared to power inherent in just letting it be known that a dormant capacity to produce them existed.

Yano was, with Haruki Mori, Michio Nagai, and Yonosuke Nagai, actively involved in the Olof Palme disarmament commission. Out of that undertaking might come better understanding of how Japan could more effectively support programs designed to achieve effective arms control/reduction.

In one of his many digressions, Yano offered his hypothesis about what happened to Japanese born in China. He mentioned that Okita had been born in Manchuria, as had Mukaibo at the Atomic Energy Commission, Sasa at the Defense Agency, retired Ambassador Ogawa, Shinkichi Eto at Tokyo University, and Yano himself. Chie Nakane, the celebrated anthropologist and author, had been born in Peking. Saeki was born on Taiwan. It was Yano's view that living in China had left an indelible mark on these people. They had lived in international communities — Han Chinese, Manchurian, and White Russian. They had learned to speak a standard brand of Japanese, unmarked by local patois or insider vocabularies. And, most important, they had been free, while young, from the constraints on social behavior inescapable while living in Japan itself.

KOICHIRO ASAKAI, FORMER AMBASSADOR
(January 25, 1983)

Koichiro Asakai, from 1958 to 1964 Japan's ambassador to Washington, and now retired, was, like Ushiba, widely admired by younger members of Japan's foreign service. As a member of the Central Liaison Office during the Occupation era, he played an indispensable role in U.S.-Japanese day-to-day relations, with his excellent command of English, great knowledge of Japan's post-World War II government apparatus, and of General MacArthur's Headquarters. In 1945, I had met Asakai in Tokyo, and have seen him periodically over the years. Okita suggested that I invite Asakai's comment on the outline.

Asakai explained that he had not advocated – had not even thought much about – the "Swedish model" while in government. Maybe "Swedish model" was, in fact, misleading shorthand.

He saw Japan's relations with the United States as having gone through three stages. First, during the MacArthur occupation the relationship was unequal. Nevertheless, it was characterized by mutual respect and trust. Second, there came a honeymoon, during the Eisenhower and early Kennedy administrations. Relations were friendly. The United States enjoyed a trade surplus. Washington told Tokyo to stop looking at trade in bilateral terms. And U.S. military preeminence, globally, was taken for granted. Third came an era of mutual frustration. Japanese suspected that the U.S. umbrella was getting to be leaky. Americans urged Japan to rearm, tended to overvalue Japan's potentials, and did not realize that an effective military build-up would require investment over 20 or 30 years. Meanwhile, economic strains were becoming intense. Now it was Japan that created the surpluses on bilateral account, and Japan was appalled at what it saw as the American reaction. Former Vice President Mondale had attacked Japanese automobile producers. Secretary of Commerce Baldrige had described Japanese culture as being inherently a nontariff barrier. Secretary of Agriculture Block had charged the Japanese system with being dedicated to protectionism. Members of Congress had proclaimed that the Japanese were a worse threat than the communists!

Asakai said that talk like this about Japan raised fundamental questions as to how Japan could deal with U.S. complaints. Trade liberalization would not solve the problem. If beef and citrus imports were totally liberalized, at a cost of, say, $600 million, doing so would reduce the trade deficit by only about 5%.

More fundamental was the question of whether it was in Japan's best interest to allow the surpluses now inescapable, it seemed, in the enormous economic interdependence of the two systems, to trap Japan in excessive subservience to the United States on issues of foreign policy and defense. Perhaps Japan should look to a much lower level of equilibrium in economic relations so as to regain its sovereign self-determination.

Tokyo, unwisely, had acquiesced in many of Washington's anti-Soviet strategies. Russians saw Japan as weak and nearby, the United States as strong and far away. For reasons of common-sense prudence, Tokyo should always be talking to Russians, should establish some degree of rapport, and should learn to know how Russians think. Japan must not confront and try to isolate the Soviet Union. Tokyo was much too ready to follow Washington's lead, in style and substance. Subservience to another country's judgment was not a necessary condition for friendship.

MICHIO NAGAI, FORMER CABINET MINISTER
(January 25, 1983)

Michio Nagai, formerly a minister of education in the Miki cabinet, was now a professor at Sophia University, a columnist for *Asahi,* and an adviser to the rector of the United Nations University in Tokyo.

Nagai spoke of the pivotal importance of the Peace Constitution to post-World War II Japan. Some Japanese had declared that Americans had written and foisted that document on a helpless and subservient Japan. General MacArthur himself had said, however, that prewar Foreign Minister Shidehara had proposed the no-war Article 9. Nagai's father was Shidehara's Vice Foreign Minister, knew him well, and admired him. Michio Nagai believed that MacArthur had told the truth about Shidehara's initiative because Shidehara was known to have said, in other settings, that the attack on Hiroshima had changed everything, that the simplest common sense should convince everyone that war was obsolete. Nagai believed that Shidehara wanted Japan's commitment to peace in its new constitution to serve Japan's interests, but also to serve the long-term interests of the whole world. In the history of the world, August 6, 1945, was for everyone a threshold event. Its impact on Japan, and the psychology and memory of the Japanese people, would never be erased.

Nagai talked about Prime Minister Nakasone, the evolution of his thinking, and his visit to Washington. Nakasone's prewar commitment to the navy had shaped, through the years, his instincts in making strategic calculations. For some reason August 6 had not affected him, or stimulated his imagination in ways that had given Yoshida, Sato, Miki, and Ohira their philosophic perspective on the true nature of war and their conviction that there should never be tampering with Japan's three nuclear principles (no possession, production, or "transit"). Nagai believed that Nakasone's recent decision to share "military" technology with the United States was unwise: considering the dual uses of any technology, it was also unnecessary. Meanwhile, public reactions to Nakasone—largely apathetic—were ambivalent, and primarily were concerned, in any case, with the likely impact of his leadership on Japan's domestic economic situation.

Nagai suspected that President Reagan had begun to understand that military spending was imposing burdens too great even for the U.S. economy. Nagai said that the condition of the Soviet economy was worse. The Japanese economy was also being threatened by budget deficits, poor administration, and an erosion in public morality manifest in the Tanaka legal process.

War was Nagai's central preoccupation. He referred, with great respect, to a study made by Frank Barnaby for the Swedish Institute for Peace Research which developed the proposition that military spending could be reduced by much greater reliance on nonprovocative defensive military technologies. He hoped that Barnaby's work foreshadowed new attitudes towards weapons.

12
CONVERSATIONS IN TOKYO WITH SOME JAPANESE ECONOMISTS

Implicit in "comprehensive security" was the notion that use of nonmilitary instruments should count in calculating contributions to mutual security requirements. However, Japanese data tabled on burden sharing, and comprehensive contributions to "comprehensive security," seemed always to be confined to budget allocations for defense appropriations and for ODA. Almost nothing quantifiable seemed to have been presented on technology transfers, cultural exchanges, creation of reserve stocks, or how the mere functioning of the Japanese system could be seen as contributing to stability/security in the Pacific region. What fragmentary aggregate data had been compiled seemed to have shown Japan's "comprehensive security" performance falling well below that of the United States, the United Kingdom, the Federal Republic of Germany, or France. Was this fair to Japan? And, if not, how could Japan's real contributions to "comprehensive security" be better quantified? Saburo Okita, Kunio Saito, Masashi Nishihara, Hiroaki Fujii, and Richard Solomon were only a few in Washington and Tokyo who wanted, and could not yet supply, the answer to that question.

MIYOHEI SHINOHARA,
INSTITUTE OF DEVELOPING ECONOMIES
(January 20 and 26, 1983)

Miyohei Shinohara, a Stanford-trained mathematical economist, was now a professor at Seikei University, a counselor of the Bank of Japan, and chairman of the widely respected Institute of Developing Economies. Takeyama, at *Nihon Keizai,* had urged Shinohara to talk with me. Before seeing him, I had sent him the outline, and had asked for his comment, in particular, on how "economic interdependence" contributed to regional security.

Shinohara said that a term like "comprehensive security" might please members of the U.S. Congress or the Japanese Diet, but the concept presented an economist difficulties. Recipient countries, normally, wanted humanitarian assistance, or aid that produced obvious mutual economic benefit more than aid that had to be explained as having "security" benefits.

The American charge of "free ride" had necessitated some Japanese reassessment of how Japan's commitment to cooperation could better synthesize use of all of its military, technological, and economic capabilities. The concept of comprehensive security had become the framework for doing this. Japan's intention to improve international *security* would focus primarily on *regional* possibilities; to contribute to international *social* solidarity, Japan would focus on *global* opportunities.

Shinohara recalled that quite recently he had made quantitative analyses of the positive and negative "boomerang" effects of Japan's economic interdependencies. For example, Japanese investment in Thai textiles, Korean steel and ship production, and other East Asian electronic production created very effective competition to Japanese producers. However, Korean ship building also created a market for Japanese engines. It was difficult — even impossible — to draw upon facts like this for quantitative proof that this dynamic was a Japanese contribution to regional security. No one had tried to make such a calculation, interesting as it might be to try.

To explore ways to present quantitatively Japan's "comprehensive security" contributions to the region through its normal economic relationships, Shinohara suggested that I enlist the help of Masao Teruyama, at MITI.

MASAO TERUYAMA,
MINISTRY FOR INTERNATIONAL TRADE
AND INDUSTRY
(January 26, 1983)

Masao Teruyama was the director of policy planning of the MITI Minister's Secretariat. Teruyama, at Shinohara's suggestion, had asked his staff to be ready to comment on various themes in my outline. Our conversation required interpretation and prolonged review of tables and charts in the Japanese language.

It had taken some considerable detective work for them to come up with a table and chart showing what might be the impact on other countries of a 30% drop in Japanese gross domestic product for 1983. The World Economic Information Service in Tokyo (WEIS) had used its computers to produce findings. For the ASEAN countries, gross domestic product (GDP) growth rate would drop by 1.9 percentage points, and for East Asia 2.7 percentage points.

I told Teruyama that the method and the projections were suggestive. They were helpful but not conclusive, I thought, in establishing clearly the positive security contribution Japan made to countries in the region merely through the efficient functioning of its economy. I suggested preparation of a table showing, country by country, population growth, GNP growth, per capita GNP growth, total Japanese trade, total Japanese investment, total U.S. trade, and total U.S. investment. Perhaps from such a chart could be extrapolated some idea of how Japanese economic behavior had been the real cause of growth processes in certain other countries, and thus the stability of their governments. Teruyama said the needed computations would be complex, quite difficult, and he feared that the results would be inconclusive. Such computations had not been tried before but would be, of course, worthwhile.

Teruyama and his staff reviewed with me various other relevant MITI data. The ideal modes for fostering economic and social development had included assisting data collection, manpower training, infrastructure consolidation, agricultural development, alternative energy sources and energy conservation, and balanced industrial development. Data on Japan's record in helping to meet these challenges were of uneven completeness. However, 1981 investment *in all forms* of economic cooperation had increased by 81% over 1980, placing Japan number two among Development Assistance Committee (DAC) countries. Japan's ODA ranked fourth among DAC countries, but dropped to thirteenth in its ODA/GNP ratio. 1981 private financial cooperation rose by 163% over 1980. Loans to multilateral organizations in 1981 rose by 840% over 1980. Export credits rose by 137%, and overseas investment by 134%.

Japan's technical cooperation in 1981 rose by 36.2% over 1980, amounting to $378 million, or 12% of total ODA. It was Japan's intention to do more, and better.

TOSHIO MATSUOKA, KEIZAI KOHO CENTER
(January 17 and 31, 1983)

Toshio Matsuoka was the editor of an excellent Japan data book brought out annually by the Keizai Koho Center, a statistical facility sponsored by the Keidanren (Japan's NAM — National Association of Manufacturers). Matsuoka was on loan from Matsushita.

I had talked in Washington with Matsuoka about his work, which I viewed with even greater respect on hearing that his book reached 160,000 users, only 10,000 of which were Japanese.

Matsuoka and his colleagues, having read my outline, asked for two weeks to try to compile the data that I wanted on Japan's technology transfers, cultural exchanges, investment in education, nuclear power projections, ODA, and "locomotive" connections. He knew that I wanted to use them in assessing the scale of Japan's use of nonmilitary instruments in carrying forward with its comprehensive security policies.

I was disappointed when Matsuoka said that he could not quickly assemble the data I wanted. He had to accept the plain fact that, as of now, most of the data simply did not exist in a form to pass on — for example, on technology transfers and cultural exchanges. An anecdotal approach was all that seemed to be possible. By way of example, he recalled that Mr. Matsushita, for personal reasons, had invested in Zambia. Finding that he could not bring home profits from that enterprise, he put his profits in new raw material-production capacity in Zambia, which did earn some transferable foreign exchange. At every stage of this procedure there was technology transfer but how could it be specified or quantified in detail? It had been discovered, moreover, that "systematic" technology transfers often ran up against shortcomings in the psychology and education of workers in recipient countries. Transfers were, in fact, ad hoc and experimental, pushed along by progression within Japan itself from higher to still higher levels of technology. A classic progression in developing countries was from production of components, to assembly, to production for the domestic market, to production for export. All this involved steady technology transfers. But how, Matsuoka asked, could it be quantified?

RYOHEI MURATA,
DIRECTOR GENERAL, ECONOMIC BUREAU
(January 27, 1983)

Ryohei Murata was director general of the Economic Affairs Bureau of the Foreign Ministry. I knew him well when he was in Japan's Washington Embassy, and saw him frequently, thereafter, until he became Japan's ambassador to the United Arab Emirates (UAE). I had not seen him during the various foreign and Tokyo assignments that brought him into the mainstream of Japan's energy and Middle East strategy calculations. We discussed "comprehensive security," in the company of Koichiro Matsuura, also a Washington alumnus and now deputy director general of the Economic Cooperation Bureau.

Over the past decade the pattern of Japan's oil imports had reflected constantly changing accommodation to political and economic change. Murata reminded me that at one time UAE ranked third after Saudi Arabia and Indonesia as a source of Japanese oil. He recalled that Iran, as a supplier of oil, had outranked Saudi Arabia, Kuwait, UAE, and Indonesia in the mid-1970s. "Comprehensive security" decisions required great elasticity in adjusting to new realities.

Revolution in Iran and the Soviet invasion of Afghanistan stimulated many new Japanese aid-giving initiatives. To Pakistan was given support of infrastructure, and assistance for refugees. Japan joined the United States and the Federal Republic of Germany in making substantial contributions of economic assistance to Turkey. Egypt was the largest recipient of Japanese aid outside of Asia: Egypt's economy was fragile, war costs had been enormous, and agriculture was in need of urgent help. Aid to Egypt illustrated Japan's commitment to the concept of comprehensive security.

Japanese aid elsewhere was on a smaller scale, but similarly motivated. Aid to the Sudan had no economic value to Japan: it helped Egypt. Justification of aid to Oman presented difficulties. Oman's per-capita GNP was very high, but the country suffered serious social problems. The volume of Japanese imports from Oman was not high: Oman's location, however, was strategic. So Japan gave it modest but significant technical assistance. Zimbabwe received substantial Japanese assistance, despite the fact that Japan had no historic ties with it and insignificant economic relations. The United Kingdom asked Japan to recognize the political importance of Zimbabwe and how the situation there could affect Zambia and South Africa: aid to Zimbabwe was another application of the strategy of comprehensive security.

Recipients of Japanese financial and technical aid in Central America included Costa Rica, El Salvador, and Honduras. Japan had intended to make a significant grant to El Salvador, but had slowed down owing to the political sensitivities of the situation. Japan extended aid to Mexico. Two years ago it extended a $10 million loan to Jamaica. Japan gave technical assistance to Cuba, but no financial aid. These activities reflected concern with "comprehensive security."

Japan did not have a long-term aid program for Thailand. However, in 1981 Japan committed in excess of $400 million to ease the refugee burden on Thailand, and to support road, airport, agriculture, village, and environmental development projects.

In Diet presentations, the government cited both humanitarian and "comprehensive security" justification for Japan's aid activities.

"Tied" and "untied" aid often carried pejorative connotation. Clarification was needed. Japan's soft loans were untied. Grant aid was tied. Technical cooperation was tied. Terms were differentiated in this way to assure efficient use.

Murata drew my attention to a 1982 Report of the Foreign Ministry in which statistics on Japan's ODA looked both good and bad. What looked good was that in 1982 Japan's ODA stood at Y941.8 billion, up from Y450.8 billion in 1976, and the GNP ratio, 0.226% in 1975, had risen to 0.340% in 1982. In 1981, only the United States, France, and the Federal Republic of Germany gave more ODA. What looked bad was Japan's aid ranking only thirteenth among the seventeen members of the DAC in ODA as a percentage of GNP.

Japan's huge budget deficits, the burden of debt servicing, and the stern disciplines of the Ministry of Finance constrained appropriation of funds needed to implement more conspicuous "comprehensive security" burden sharing.

A March 31, 1981 Resolution on Economic Cooperation of the Diet's Foreign Affairs Committee contained this reminder of concern over war:

> . . . to abstain from extending such economic and technical cooperation that will be utilized for the military purposes, as in the case of military facilities.[11]

Back in 1978, the same committee adopted a prior resolution foreshadowing "comprehensive security":

> Basing on the spirit of our Constitution which promulgated perpetual peace and international concord, the Government shall . . . expand its official development assistance by way of more than doubling it in the coming five years. . . .[12]

This goal was surpassed.

13
CONVERSATIONS IN TOKYO WITH SOME WEAPONS SPECIALISTS

The Inoki Report deplored grossly disproportionate expenditure on personnel at the expense of procurement, which created "absolute weakness of arms and equipment both in quantity and quality."[13] The report said that studying arms systems and improving software would help Japan to remedy matters while still keeping defense spending at a quite low level. Saburo Okita, Hiroaki Fujii, Kenichi Ito, and many others referred me to a literature in Japanese that dealt with possibilities. As new or improved military technologies were compared, expected mission was, of course, crucial: what was better or worse was relevant only to "what for?" Hiroshi Doi and some members of the American Embassy staff were particularly interesting because they knew the technologies and were ready to speculate on what should be Japan's military mission. They assumed that I was familiar with Japan's present force structure, and Japan's force build-up plans. From time to time, conversation was interrupted as I refreshed my memory by consulting the treatment of "building the defense" in the 1981 issue of *Asian Security,* an authoritative book brought out annually by the Research Institute for Peace and Security, and by consulting the Japan entry in the IISS (International Institute for Strategic Studies) *Military Balance 1983-1984.* For reference, I include these extracts, even though by now some details are out of date:

BUILDING THE DEFENSE*

As has already been said, the "Defense Plan Outline" was formulated in October 1976, and from that time the plans have been on an annual basis. One reason for this was that the plan was merely an outline showing the

---

*From Research Institute for Peace and Security, *Asian Security 1981,* (Tokyo: 1981), pp. 159-162, with permission.

number of units as a target. The main reason, however, was that in the face of the large expenditures involved over a period of several years, the Defense Agency would have had difficulty in obtaining governmental approval so far in advance, even in general terms, and found that a single-year system was more suitable for obtaining the desired budget allocations.

An annual system was thus chosen for planning and funding, but nonetheless a larger framework proved necessary. Consequently, 1978 saw the initiation of a "medium-term defense build-up plan" system. The work was done at the Defense Agency level and was not subject to National Defense Council approval. The system called for the formulation every three years of a rolling five-year plan that would take effect two years after formulation, a budget requested annually. The 1978 medium-term defense build-up plan was to cover the years FY 1980 to FY 1984, to be followed by a 1981 plan for FY 1983 to FY 1987. A review was allowed for the intervening years between plans so that any necessary modifications could be made. The 1978 plan, which was based on the premise that expenditures for FY 1984 would rise to a level of 1% of GNP from the FY 1979 rate of 0.9%, set aside Y2,700 billion ($12.3 billion) to Y2,800 billion ($12.7 billion) for the purchase of equipment which included the following principal items:

• GSDF: Tanks, 301 (to be increased to approximately 1,130); 155-mm SP howitzers, 140; 203-mm SP howitzers, 40; armored vehicles, approximately 40; armored cars, 70; 2 HAWK SAM for AA Groups, to be replaced by improved HAWK SAM.

• MSDF: GM destroyers, 2; destroyers, 10; destroyer escorts, 4 (at end of 1978 medium-term plan); ASW ships to total 58, of which 35 are to be GM equipped; diesel submarines, 5 (14 by end of plan); mine sweepers, 11 (40 by end of plan); submarine rescue ship, oceanographic research ship, supply ship, 1 each. In all, 70,160 tons; ASW patrol aircraft, 37; ASW helicopters for ships, 28; mine-sweeping helicopters, 6.

• ASDF: Interceptors, 77; close support fighters, 13; EW planes, 4 (94 combat aircraft, to be increased to 340 by end of plan); advanced trainers, 23.

If all this equipment was procured, the strengths would still not reach the levels of naval ships and combat aircraft shown in the attached table of the "Defense Plan Outline." MSDF vessels would number 58 as against 60; submarines 14 (16); combat aircraft 180 (220), a shortfall of 40 (10 large ASW aircraft, 10 land-based ASW helicopters, 10 ship-borne ASW helicopters, and 10 mine-sweeping helicopters). ASDF combat aircraft would be 340 (430), a gap of 90 (30 interceptors, 30 close support fighters, 20 reconnaissance aircraft, and 10 transports).

What are the prospects for the 1978 plan (1980–1984)? The percentage of GNP, projected to be 0.92% for FY 1980 and 0.94% for FY 1981, remained at 0.9%, with no indications as to when the figure of 1% can be reached. It is, therefore, doubtful whether the plan can be brought forward by one year as requested by the United States or whether the original plan can be fully implemented. The FY 1981 defense budget (April 1981–March 1982) shows that appropriations for the purchase of major operational equipment have been included, in deference to American wishes, but those for rear support remain markedly inadequate. The cost of equipment has also gone up sharply, not only in Japan but elsewhere, particularly where complex electronics are concerned. Furthermore, SDF equipment manufactured domestically or under license has tended to be very expensive indeed because production runs are short.

As of March 1980, the SDF manpower establishment figures and the actual strengths excluding civilians were:

- GSDF: 180,000 (155,131)

- MSDF: 42,278 (40,816)

- ASDF: 45,492 (44,066)

- Total: 267,853 (240,096)

The major equipment levels were:

- GSDF: 830 tanks; 560 armored cars; 860 field guns; 1,860 mortars; 1,330 recoilless guns; 330 antiaircraft guns; 70 rocket launchers; 311 liaison, reconnaissance, and transport aircraft.

- MSDF: 48 escorts (104,000 tons); 14 submarines (24,000 tons); 40 mine warfare vessels (16,000 tons); 6 amphibious ships (11,000 tons); 104 large and small ASW aircraft; 63 ASW helicopters; 7 mine sweeping helicopters.

- ASDF: 333 interceptors; 39 support fighters; 30 transports.

MAJOR GENERAL HIROSHI DOI, DEFENSE ACADEMY (January 29, 1983)

Major General Hiroshi Doi, author of *Defense of Japan by Hedgehog Armament,* was a member of the faculty of the National Defense Academy at Yokosuka. From 1967 to 1971 Doi was Japan's defense attaché at its Washington embassy.

Much that Doi said about alliance with the United States, the capabilities and vulnerabilities of the Soviet Union, and Japan's military potentials echoed what had been said by Nishihara, Sakonjo, and many other Japanese. However, his book had begun with a prologue on missile warfare and ended

JAPAN

Population: 119,400,000.
Military service: voluntary.
Total armed forces: 241,000 (ceiling 270,184).
Est GNP 1981: yen 251,289 bn ($1,104,494 bn). 1982: 263,983 bn ($1,057.616 bn).
Est def exp 1981: yen 2,448.01 bn ($10.76 bn). 1982: yen 2,586.1 bn ($10.36 bn).
GNP growth 1981: 2.7%. 1982: 2.4%
Inflation 1981: 4.9%. 1982: 2.7%
$1 = yen 227.515 (1981), 249.602 (1982).

Army: 156,000.
5 Army HQ.
1 armd div.
12 inf divs (7,000 or 9,000 men each).
2 composite bdes.
1 AB bde.
1 arty bde, 2 arty gps; 8 SAM gps (each of 4 btys).
1 sigs bde.
5 engr bdes.
1 trg bde, 2 trg regts.
Army Aviation:
1 hel bde (2 bns) and 5 Gp HQ with 24 sqns/dets.
AFV: 560 Type 61, 390 Type 74 MBT; 425 Type 60, 115 Type 73 APC.
Arty: 380 105mm, 330 155mm incl Type 74 and 75 SP, 70 203mm guns/how; 50 Type 30 SSM; 800 81mm, 560 107mm mor (some SP); 40 Type 75 SP 130mm MRL.
ATK: 1,400 75mm, *Carl Gustav* 84mm, 106mm (incl Type 60 SP) RCL; 240 Type 64, 25 Type 79 ATGW.
AD: 170 35mm twin, 37mm, 40mm incl M-42 SP, 75mm AA guns; 2 Type 81 *Tan*, 144 HAWK, 84 *Improved* HAWK SAM.
Air: some 28 ac and 370 hel: 20 LR-1, 2 TL-1, 10 L-19 ac; 2 AH-1S, 56 KV-107, 80 UH-1H, 65 UH-1B, 36 TH-55, 139 OH-6J/D hel.
(On order: 84 Type 74 MBT; 9 Type 73 APC; 34 Type 75 155mm, 19 M-110A2 203mm SP how; 8 Type 75 130mm MRL; 9 Type 79, *MAT* ATGW; 221 84mm RCL; 49 *Stinger*, 8 Type 81 *Tan* launchers, 48 *Improved* HAWK SAM; 1 LR-1 ac; 6 OH-6D, 5 UH-1H, 12 *TOW*-armed AH-1S hel.)

RESERVES: 41,000.

Navy: 42,000 (including naval air).
14 submarines: 4 *Yushio*, 7 *Uzushio*, 3 *Asashio*.
31 destroyers: 2 *Shirane* with *Sea Sparrow* SAM, 1 × 8 ASROC ASW msl launcher, 3 ASW hel; 2 *Haruna* with 1 × 8 ASROC, 3 ASW hel; 2 *Hatsuyuki* with 2 × 4 *Har-poon* SSM, 1 *Sea Sparrow*, 1 × 8 ASROC, 1 ASW hel; 3 *Tachikaze* with *Tartar/Standard* SAM, 1 × 8 ASROC; 1 *Amatsukaze* with 1 *Standard* SAM, 1 × 8 ASROC; 4 *Takatsuki* with 1 × 8 ASROC; 6 *Yamagumo* with 1 × 8 ASROC; 3 *Minegumo* with 1 × 8 ASROC; 2 *Akizuki*; 3 *Murasame*; 3 *Ayanami*.
17 frigates: 1 *Yubari*; 1 *Ishikari* with 2 × 4 *Harpoon* SSM; 11 *Chikugo* with 1 × 8 ASROC; 4 *Isuzu*.
5 large patrol craft: 3 *Mizutori*, 2 *Umitaka*.
5 FAC(T).

9 coastal patrol craft(.
3 MCM spt ships, 31 coastal minesweepers (9 *Hat-sushima*, 19 *Takami*, 3 *Kasado)*, 6 *Nanago* MCM boats.
1 *Katori*, 2 *Ayanami* trg, 1 *Azuma* trg spt, 5 utility ships incl 1 *Harukaze*.
6 LST (3 *Miura*, 3 *Atsumi*); 2 LSU. 37 landing craft.

Bases: Yokosuka, Kure, Sasebo, Maizuru, Ominato.

NAVAL AIR ARM: (11,000); 93 combat ac, 62 combat hel. 6 Air Wings.
8 MR sqn with 6 P-3C, 58 P-2J, 13 S2F-1, 16 PS-1.
6 ASW hel sqns with 55 HSS-2.
1 MCM hel sqn with 7 KV-107.
1 tpt sqn with 4 YS-11M, 1 B-65.
1 utility sqn with 3 UP-2J.
1 test sqn with 2 P-3C, 2 P-2J, 2 P-2H, 1 UC-90 ac; 3 HSS-2A/B hel.
7 SAR flts with 8 US-1 ac, 6 S-61A, 8 S-62B hel.
5 trg sqns with 6 YS-11T, 15 TC-90, 14 B-65, 32 KM-2, 19 P-2J, 3 T-34A ac; 3 OH-6J, 6 Bell 47G, 11 HSS-2 hel.
(On order: 3 *Yushio* subs; 1 4,500-ton, 10 *Hatsuyuki* destroyers; 1 *Yubari* frigate; 2 *Hatsushima* MCM; 17 P-3C, 2 KM-2, 3 TC-90 ac; 14 HSS-2B, 5 S-61A, 20 H-6D hel; 24 *Harpoon* SSM, 3 Mk 15 *Phalanx* 20mm antiship msl defence systems.)

RESERVES: 600.

Air Force: 43,000; some 280 combat aircraft.
6 combat air wings; 1 combat air gp; 1 recce sqn.
3 FGA sqns with 56 F-1.
11 interceptor sqns: 1 with some 20 F-15J/DJ (2nd form-ing), 4 T-33A; 6 with 112 F-4EJ; 3 with 61 F-104J.
Air Recce Group: 1 recce sqn with 12 RF-4EJ.
1 aggressor trg sqn with 5 T-2, 2 T-33.
1 tactical tpt wing of 3 sqns with 25 C-1, 6 YS-11.
1 SAR wing (9 dets) with MU-2 ac; 29 KV-107 hel.
1 air test wing with 2 F-4EJ, 5 F-15J, F-104J/DJ, 2 T-1, 6 T-2, 2 T-3, T-33A, C-1, 2 E-2C, YS-11.
1 air traffic control and weather wing with YS-11, MU-2J, T-33A.
5 trg wings: 10 sqns with 40 T-1A/B, 59 T-2, 44 T-3, 50 T-33A.
AAM: *Sparrow, Falcon, Sidewinder.*
Air Defence:
3 aircraft control and warning wings and 1 group with 28 control and warning sites.
6 SAM gps: 19 sqns with 180 *Nike-J*.
(On order: 51 F-15J, 6 F-15DJ, 5 F-1 fighters, 4 C-130H tpt, 12 T-2 trg, 6 E-2C AEW ac; 1 V-107 hel; 5 Type 81 *Tan* SAM launchers.)

Para-Military Forces: Coast Guard: 42 large patrol vessels, 5 with 1 hel; 47 med, 19 small, 220 coastal patrol vessels (204(); 1 C-130HMP, 5 YS-11, 2 Skyvan, 2 *King Air* ac, 5 Bell 212 hel.
(On order: 1 large, 2 med, 1 coastal patrol craft.)

From the International Institute for Strategic Studies, *The Military Balance 1983-1984,* (London: 1983), pp. 92-93, with permission.

with an epilogue strongly endorsing a comprehensive approach to Japan's strategic requirements. Because he wrote and talked as a weapons analyst, I found many of his observations of special interest.

Doi developed his views, he explained, from an initial conviction that Japan's mission according to its Constitution should be to defend Japan only. The Suzuki/Nakasone commitments to defend sea-lanes had been a departure, according to Doi, from that principle. It was Doi's opinion that Japan should, instead, be developing the tactical capability to deal with Soviet naval and air forces in the Seas of Japan/Okhotsk, within the Straits, and along the coastlines. To be ready for combat in that area should be the limit of Japan's intention. The strategic capabilities of Soviet Backfires, submarines, and SS-20s should be regarded as the strategic responsibility of the United States: in dealing with those Soviet capabilities, Japan's role could be only supportive to the United States.

Suzuki and Nakasone had described the United States as an ally: Doi approved. However, the alliance was one-sided, and rightly so. If the United States asked Japan to close the Straits because it was fighting the Soviet Union in, for example, the Middle East, Japan would have to refuse, knowing that Soviet retaliation would be against Japan's homeland, while the U.S. homeland, being far distant, would likely be spared. Japan's military responsibility should be to defend Japan only, and only for Japanese reasons.

France was a useful model of a country that could be pro-Western but not committed to NATO. France was not a perfect model for Japan because Japan rejected the nuclear component in the French prototype. Public sentiment was utterly opposed to nuclear weapons: memory of Hiroshima was still vivid. Moreover, to acquire many weapons would be astronomically expensive. Since none should ever be ground based, acquiring a few would mean mounting them in Sea Launched Ballistic Missiles (SLBMs). Doi opposed any Japanese possession of nuclear weapons, ever.

Use of missiles by Egypt on the sea in 1967, by the United Kingdom and Argentina in the battle for the Falklands, and by the Israelis in Lebanon offered instructive lessons of how technology affects tactics. Before Pearl Harbor the battleship was the queen of naval power. Thereafter came the aircraft carrier. Now the need was for high-speed missile-carrying boats. They, rather than destroyers, were what was needed in the Sea of Japan, and for defense of the Straits and coastlines. The navy, but also the ground forces and the air force, should become much more heavily armed with missiles. For this to be accomplished, the air force did not need more planes, only some reconfiguration of how many squadrons should be interceptors and how many should be missile-armed support squadrons. Doi would favor Japan's retaining its thirteen squadrons, but reducing from ten the interceptors and increasing from three the missile-armed support squadrons. Ground forces, too, should cut back on tank procurement — at $1.6 million a copy — to acquire antitank and coastal defense surface-to-surface missile systems. Some advocated acquisition of missiles as an economy measure, but not Doi. They could be more expensive, initially, but would not be over time, and they were much more efficient.

Missiles were not the sole, all-purpose, and infallible answer to Japan's "defense only" requirements: their value should not be exaggerated. The requirement for surface-to-air missiles (SAMs) will be very large. Missiles could shoot down your own planes. Used over your own territory they could fall on friendly targets. Their rate of obsolescense was high. They were difficult to produce at first. Other high-technology weapons systems had to be developed or improved, like electronic countermeasures and electronic counter-countermeasures. Laser and optic fiber technology is advanced in Japan, but military applications lie some distance down the road. Meanwhile, the investment in missiles, notwithstanding their imperfections, should be of very high priority.

Japan produced an excellent ASM-1 (air-to-surface missile) probably better than the French Exocet, with greater accuracy and a longer range. Plans were afoot to arm the F-1 and the F-4 with ASM-1. This missile was also being modified to surface-to-surface (SSM) for use by Japanese ground forces, which already deploy the HAWK. Japan produced the 140-kilometer-range antiaircraft NIKE (SAM) under license. Japan bought and armed its F-15s with the 10 kilometer-range air-to-air missile (AAM) Sidewinder and the 30-40 kilometer-range AAM Sparrow.

Soviet bombers carried sophisticated missiles. The Backfire could launch its missiles 150–200 kilometers from target. Japanese interceptors could go after the Backfire but not the Backfire missiles.

Doi proposed that Japan should devote 1.7% of its GNP to meet its defense needs. This would match Canada's defense/GNP ratio.

U.S. MILITARY STAFF (January 26 and 31, 1983)

Ambassador Mansfield's embassy staff in Tokyo included many highly experienced foreign service and military officers with command of the Japanese language and extraordinary familiarity with Japanese psychology and Japan's cultural inheritance. I found them to be less ready to talk about negotiations on defense matters than many of the Japanese I talked with or many of the Americans I had interviewed back in Washington. Nevertheless, their comments on certain themes of my outline were illuminating.

They believed that "knowledge is power" and "knowledge as deterrence" were themes that would appeal to Prime Minister Nakasone. "Hedgehog" was application of science and technology—especially information technology—to Japan's defense requirements. Investment in Japanese aircraft, destroyers, and submarines might impress the Free World with the sincerity of Japan's burden-sharing intention. It would not scare the Russians. A real Japanese commitment to create new, or to improve known, technologies might, on the other hand, really frighten Moscow.

The "AWACS concept" was attractive, as far as it went. But there were other unmentioned possibilities for keeping a watch on the region. Satellite technology was excellent, but satellites could be shot down. Simpler avionics and electronic warfare technologies were natural fields for which Japan's scientific and engineering skills could be enlisted. Hiroshi Doi's stress on missile potentials was constructive. However, it was unwise to become overcommitted to any single formula: the Soviet Union was improving its own antimissile technologies. The ultimate objective, strategically, was to remove vulnerable, fallible man from military operations. There was some movement towards the "AWACS concept": BADGE was being upgraded so that it could, now hardened significantly, service both the Japanese navy and Japan's ground forces.

Some embassy personnel observed that the outline failed to bring out how badly Japan presented what it was really doing about security: it had no skill in projecting an attractive image of itself. Others had to make the case for Japan. And, as to the appetite for knowledge, it was greater and more refined where economics was involved than where diplomatic opportunity presented itself. Furthermore, Japan was often very slow in responding to a need to pick up the slack, as, for example, in making urgently needed supplementary contributions to World Bank resources.

In comprehensive security there were hints of Japan's ceaseless and haunting sense of danger. Fear of earthquakes was an example. Japan's Self Defense Forces carried out regular exercises to deal with the possibly disastrous social and environmental consequences of violent natural upheavals. Japan's literature on earthquakes was read with obsessive interest. Some believed that events like the 1923 Yokohama earthquake/fire ran in sixty-year cycles: thus, 1983 presented portentous possibilities. Fear of earthquakes had influenced Tokyo's architects and housing authorities, but not paralyzed them. And the possibility of volcanic eruptions had caused soothsayers to forecast an explosion of Fuji tearing away one side, thus activating a colossal flow of destructive lava towards Sagami Bay. Japan scrupulously measured all volcanic and earthquake activity, even the smallest tremors.

In the Japanese imagination there was always the possibility of helpless acceptance of disaster. Something like the same psychology of unrelievable vulnerability affected Japan's feelings about its dependence on Japan's farmers. Defending them might not be prompted so much by economic considerations, or even by the importance of the farmer's vote to various political parties and factions. What was involved was ultimate survival.

14
CONVERSATIONS IN TOKYO WITH SOME PRIME MINISTERS: PAST AND "FUTURE"

A prime minister's perspective differs from that of any member of his cabinet, each of whom is necessarily a special pleader. Takeo Miki, prime minister following the Sato era, left a lasting mark on thinking about what is now called the concept of comprehensive security. During Miki's administration the 1% ceiling on defense spending became a firm guideline. Guidelines that "prohibited" sales of military equipment to countries condemned by the United Nations, countries at war, and countries adjacent to conflict areas (but in actual practice applicable to all countries) were tightened. Having held various cabinet portfolios before becoming prime minister, his familiarity with government operations was wide. Prime Minister Nakasone's defense minister was a member of the Miki faction in the LDP. Kiichi Miyazawa was cabinet secretary for Prime Minister Suzuki, having been minister for planning, for foreign affairs, and for international trade and industry. He was being groomed for leadership of the strong Ohira/Suzuki faction. Many Japanese foresaw his becoming prime minister following Prime Minister Nakasone, despite the present modesty of his political demeanor. Both talked at length with me about "comprehensive security."

KIICHI MIYAZAWA, FORMER CABINET MINISTER
(January 28, 1983)

Kiichi Miyazawa was minister for planning in the Sato Cabinet when I first met him, almost twenty years ago. Subsequently, he was Japan's minister for trade and industry during the Nixon administration, when textiles grievously troubled U.S.-Japanese relations, and he was minister for foreign affairs during the Ford administration. Miyazawa's mastery of English was unique among Japanese political personalities. Not only did he speak with fluency, he was able, it seemed, to gain instant command of Washington's insider jargon. I had never heard the term "sub-rocs" before he talked with me about them years ago. Still, with all of his linguistic proficiency,

Miyazawa's conversational style was lean, precise, and, in its brevity, suggestive rather than in any way didactic.

Miyazawa had read and made notes on the outline. There was appeal, he said, in the idea that Japan should acquire AWACS, and help to finance a Southeast Asian nonmilitary coast guard. Doing things like that could contribute to regional security and would be consistent with Japan's "defense only" intentions. Doing such things might also improve Japan's image.

What the outline had said about "threat" raised questions. Why did Japan fear, less than the United States, attack by the Soviet Union? Why was this so, despite Russia's geographic proximity, still vivid and powerful memories of war, and knowledge that Russia was now building up enormous Backfire and missile capabilities quite nearby?

One reason was that use of Russia's weapons capability, though great, would be restrained by many weaknesses in the Soviet system. The economy was in trouble. The invasion of Afghanistan was not a success. Poland symbolized Russian difficulties in Eastern Europe.

Another reason was that it was not Japan's policy to quarrel with countries whose ideas and values differed from Japan's — on that account alone. Japan's foreign relations were shaped by pragmatic considerations, but also by a wish to defend, within constitutional limits, certain basic values that Japan shares with the industrialized democracies.

There were other factors: Japan was constantly endangered by earthquakes. Historically, their injury to Japan had been enormous. But Japan could do nothing to control earthquakes. So, Japanese did not let themselves become obsessed with worry. In 1904, Japan worried about Russia. At that time, they knew that they could do something. They fought, and won, a war. Today the military powers of the Soviet Union compared to Japan were absolutely overwhelming. There was nothing the Japanese people could imagine doing to deal with that capability. Consequently, when Moscow deployed and redeployed SS-20s, Backfires, or the Minsk, Japan just remained impervious to the signals Moscow might be intending to transmit.

Miyazawa deeply hoped that Japanese behavior would not cause the United States to withdraw its forces from Japan. Were that to happen, Japan would likely feel very insecure: the U.S. umbrella did, of course, contribute to Japan's sense of safety. And the stationing of F-16s at Mizawa, together with the recent unexcited reception of the *Enterprise,* showed Japan's readiness to accept the American umbrella.

However, threat and threat response presented subtle and painful difficulties. Japan excluded from its logic of strategic necessity any benefit from nuclear war-making. Nevertheless, Japan had to acknowledge that the American capability deterred the Soviet Union from striking out. Consequently, Japan did depend, in reality, on the U.S. nuclear capability. This fact presented the Japanese people with a dilemma. They were fiercely attached to their three nuclear principles. However, in the people's imagination, both the United States and the Soviet Union were confronting each other "out there," with the possibility that American intercontinental ballistic missiles (ICBMs) might one day overfly Japan, but still not encroach on Japanese territory, and thus contravene the three principles. With this mindset, the issue of "no first use" presented very touchy difficulties. How could Japan, realistically, oppose "first use" and remain beneficiary of a security umbrella furnished by a United States that did not renounce that option? Japan should not be guilty of such inconsistency.

Reverting to other themes in the outline, Miyazawa concurred in the proposition that *lack* of articulated common purpose was, often, a source of safety. This was a subtle concept that many would find hard to understand. Nevertheless, the proposition accorded with reality.

Miyazawa also accepted fully the propriety and accuracy of the contention that the mere functioning of a dynamic Japanese economy had contributed to growth, stability, and the legitimacy of government leadership in the Pacific region. However, this had not been Japan's design, only an unintended result. It reflected no special virtue, and no praise was deserved. The real question was what more should Japan do?

I suggested that there could be some virtue in "creative egocentrism," if, as in the case of Japan, the marriage of Confucian ethical and aesthetic values with Western science and technology became a model emulated by others.

Miyazawa found intriguing and important the outline's treatment of the concept that for Japan "knowledge is power." But was this conviction uniquely Japanese? It was true, perhaps, that Confucianism was knowledge-oriented and imposed useful disciplines. Miyazawa recalled, and wrote down, an ancient Chinese aphorism:

> To think, without learning, is wayward;
> To learn, without thinking, yields only obscurity.

Miyazawa believed that Prime Minister Nakasone might profit from reading the "knowledge as deterrence" part of the outline. It contained some useful ideas. But, Miyazawa went on, why was AWACS, actually, so much better than E-2C? I told him. He then asked why Japan had turned it down. I replied that it was because AWACS could stay in the air four times longer than the E-2C and because it had much greater "battle-management" capability. Japanese negotiators concluded that having it would be inconsistent with "defense only." Miyazawa was thoughtfully amused.

Miyazawa did not now worry much about South Korea's acquisition of nuclear weapons. There would be something to worry about if North Korea got one first.

In the context of U.S.-Japan defense arrangements, Japan would have, Miyazawa sadly observed, great — perhaps impossible — difficulty in refuting "free ride." Japan would do its best to meet its targets on time, but might not achieve them all by 1987. Contracts would have been let, however, and deliveries would be made a little later, especially ships. Even after Japan had reached its targets, doing so would not have met Washington's assessment of what were Japan's air-cover and sea-lane-protection requirements. Doing what it would do might not answer the charge of "free ride," but maybe charges would be less harsh, and Washington might be given basis for saying Japan was on its way.

Miyazawa urged me to delete the final paragraph of the outline: the possibility that Japan would possess nuclear weapons was so remote as to be not worth mentioning. If I had to mention the theoretical possibility, then I should reject the likelihood and give all the persuasive reasons known to everyone for making that judgment.

TAKEO MIKI, FORMER PRIME MINISTER
(January 30, 1983)

Saburo Okita was present at the interview and dinner with Takeo Miki, which took place at his home. Taking the initiative, Miki asked what Americans said about the *Comprehensive National Security Report*? I responded that Americans were prone to focus on day-to-day specific problems, and seldom talked about "comprehensive security" at all. Few of those who did talk about it had read the report. Of those very few who had read the report, most considered it to be an interesting document which raised questions as to whether it was an alibi for inaction on security questions or a meaningful new prescription for national behavior.

Miki retorted that the concept was not an alibi. Security was, for Japan, something clearly comprehensive. Japan's dependence on imported food, energy, and raw materials created great vulnerabilities (see Appendix I). Japan's existence depended vitally on stable foreign economic relations. No Japanese could disagree. As to military defense, Japan must have, of course, an adequate military capability, but great military strength was not the most important requirement for Japan's security.

Miki said that military build-up targets had been agreed to about seven years ago. They were adequate. Japan's forward movement towards meeting them would be, of course, constrained to some extent by financial considerations. However, defense spending was increasing every year. If the 6.5% 1983 increase was insufficient, it might have to be increased later on, or target dates pushed back a little. It was important for Japan to be clear about, and to live up to, its commitments.

A basic tenet of Japanese policy was that no country was an "enemy." Japan must be on guard, of course, but short of direct confrontation Japan would not treat the Soviet Union as an enemy country. To prepare for war against the Soviet Union would not be a sensible strategy for Japan. Unless the Soviet Union made some gross miscalculation, Japan would never need to actually make use of its military forces.

Okita recalled that Henry Kissinger had said that the Soviet Union only understood power, and construed weapons deficiencies to be a sign of weakness. Was this, Okita asked, a view shared by most Americans? It was, I replied, the view of President Reagan and his defense secretary.

Recalling themes in the Inoki Report, Okita saw need for Japan to contribute more substantially to easing North-South tensions. Instead of putting too much into defense spending, Japan should increase the percentage of its GNP available to help LDCs, particularly in the Pacific region. Affluent countries had been seriously remiss in neglecting the problems of the poor countries. Consequences could be quite dangerous. Japan's share in carrying common burdens might be most effective by helping to reduce that threat to security. Doing so might not, unfortunately, help much in silencing charges of "free ride."

Miki recalled that "free ride" was not a new term. Dean Rusk had used it when Miki was foreign minister. At that time, Miki had responded with an expression of gratitude for all that the United States had done for Japan since World War II, and pointed out that Japan had tried to make some compensation. United States military installations had been created on Japanese soil. Japan helped to maintain them. United States strategic potentials — as well as prestige — were enhanced.

Miki went on to say that during the Johnson/Rusk era the U.S. economy was stronger. Now possible breakdown of the world economy was the greatest of all threats to world security. And that threat was not to be removed by focusing on questions like Japan's imports of beef and citrus fruits, where political considerations were, in any case, the real issue. For Americans, resolution of the beef and citrus fruit question tested fairness. For Japanese, the financial cost would not be large — say $300 million — but in the imagination of the Japanese farmer a concession on beef and citrus fruit would foreshadow similar treatment for rice, which was a very large issue in Japanese political, social, and economic calculation. Okita recalled that Senator Russell Long had once argued that it was wrong for Japan to produce rice: Japanese farmers were terrified. Miki said that agricultural liberalization could not be achieved overnight. However, targets could be set, and liberalization should be achieved gradually.

At times of media exaggeration of economic controversy, some said Japan faced the dilemma of adherence to or separation from alliance with the United States. Actually, Miki said, Japan would never face that dilemma. Japan would always preserve a close association with the United States. In any war Japan would, necessarily, be involved. However, Japan's special role should be to help to prevent war, and to try to create an international climate where wars became less and less likely. The United States, Western Europe, and Japan should, together, use friendly persuasion, and a combination of pressures and inducements to forestall war.

Miki observed that a recurring Japanese difficulty in discussing strategic questions with Americans was Washington's stress on its global responsibilities. Japan's concerns, in contrast, were limited to Japan and its neighborhood. Prime Minister Nakasone's Washington visit seemed to have succeeded in making possible very useful conversations on both trade and defense questions. Particularly welcome was the apparent absence of evasion and doubletalk. Only the overtones of what Prime Minister Nakasone had said during his *Washington Post* interview had stimulated critical comment by the Japanese press. Many problems remained unresolved, of course, but there was now an improved atmosphere, more open and reasonable.

15
CONVERSATIONS WITH SOME SCHOLARS, AMBASSADORS, AND JOURNALISTS

Towards the end of the hours I spent scheduling interviews in Tokyo and in Hongkong I sought out comment from those I knew to be professionally preoccupied with Japan, but who were not primarily interested in "comprehensive security," as such. To faculty members at the United Nations University in Tokyo I was indebted for frank comment on how Japan's deep but unspoken fears, including fear of Russia, could, one day, burst forth in a radical swing to the right — and how declining confidence in the power and wisdom of the United States could contribute to that unwanted calamity.

The Thai ambassador to Japan drew attention to how, within ASEAN, there were differing memories of Japanese behavior during World War II. Thai memories were not ugly, as was the case for the Philippines, Malaysia, and Singapore; Japan was allied to Thailand. And because Thai relations with Japan had been continuous and very close for many decades, Bangkok could stand apart from Singapore and Malaysia when with surprise and delight the spectacle of Japan had caused them to embrace "look East" strategies.

The Indonesian Ambassador to Japan, now writing an intellectual history of Japan, expressed hope that a comprehensive transformation of the Japanese mind, like that which took place with Japan's sixth-century acceptance of Confucian and Buddhist values, could now help to prepare Japan for accepting responsibilities in a reshaping of the East Asian and Pacific community upon which Japan's own survival could well depend. Indonesia's ambassador made melancholy reference to Spengler, in deploring the materialism, runaway individualism, and absence of collective purpose among leaders of the West.

The Philippines' ambassador to Japan regretted Japan's failure to conceptualize its great opportunities in the region, anticipated close collaboration between Tokyo and Washington on security matters, and praised President Reagan's policy priorities.

My final two interviews were with journalists, in Hongkong. Nayan Chanda rightly objected to neglect of Vietnam. His attempt to remedy the oversight became, in microcosm, one of the most convincing case studies I heard of how Tokyo, as a practical matter, could go about translating, quietly and with no fanfare, the concept of comprehensive security into practical program. Derek Davies, from the perspective of Hongkong and his editorial offices there, offered me the most systematic comment I heard from anyone, except perhaps Nishihara and Miyazawa, on all of the themes of the outline. He ended his comment with a bold suggestion, only alluded to most delicately by anyone else. If Andropov were as intelligent as advertised, and became alerted to signs of panic in the ongoing disputes between American and Japanese negotiators, he might concoct a formula for economic cooperation with Tokyo: a Japan outraged because wounded by insulting demands for capitulation to Washington's demands, economic and defense, might be tempted to look to Siberia for new frontiers. Davies, as always, had a refreshing capacity to remind us, boldly, that what governments said was not always as good a clue to future possibilities as what ordinary people come to feel is the real outlook for their welfare, safety, and dignity. In the end, people, in their indirect, tortured, but insistent way, do tell governments what they must do, sometimes misguidedly.

UNITED NATIONS UNIVERSITY SCHOLARS
(January 15 and 30, 1983)

At the United Nations University in Tokyo there was a community of international scholars studying peace and conflict resolution; the global economy; environment, resources, and other critical elements in the development process; historical and cultural factors in global interdependence; and the impact on North-South relations of trends in science and technology. The rector and his colleagues were conscious of the global constituency they served. Their comments on Japan, voiced diffidently and always in a strictly personal capacity, revealed obvious familiarity with crosscurrents of opinion in the Japanese intellectual community. Some were unusually suggestive.

Japan's forebodings about its vulnerabilities should not lightly be brushed aside. There was deep fear of the Soviet Union which was seldom talked about. There was fear of strong-arm pressure by the United States, which if carried too far would increase Japan's own vulnerabilities, not reduce them. There was fear of subordination. There was fear of recurrence of the racism inherent in the fact that the Americans used the atomic bomb on Japanese, but might not have used it on Europeans. Behind Japan's appearance of great stability and its omnidirectional diplomatic smiles lay fears that could erupt with sudden and passionate volatility. What seemed to be LDP stubbornness on issues like beef and citrus fruits reflected, in part, the LDP need to retain the support of the Japanese farmer, but, more fundamentally, it reflected determination to put a lid on growth of support for Japan's extreme right. The extreme right was Japan's loose cannon.

Japan had caught up with the United States and Western Europe. Others in the East Asia region were now catching up with Japan. The United States-Japan alliance still appeared to remain the pivotal factor in strategic calculation of all other countries in the region. However, what were the real prospects for the restructuring of a strong and competitive American economy upon which the present trustworthy alliance depended? What would be the real strength of the United States thirty years hence? How could the United States and Japan really complement each other's power, in the next few years, even if they set out to do so? Southeast Asia now stood by, watching: Southeast Asia would be affected. How might Southeast Asia try, one day, to accommodate to a steadily declining American participation in solving the real problems of Southeast Asia, for which possession of weapons by them or even by the United States was, by and large, irrelevant?

Prime Minister Nakasone might call for both Upper and Lower House elections before the end of 1983. His Washington visit was intended to clear away some debris so that he could move along towards forging an independent Japanese national policy. The outcome of those elections would determine whether the government was given a mandate to pursue peace or rearmament.

WICHIAN WATANAKUN, THAI AMBASSADOR
(February 1, 1983)

Wichian Watanakun was Thailand's ambassador in Japan, having previously been the Thai ambassador to the United Nations in Geneva and to France. During his Tokyo tour he had worked with five Japanese foreign ministers, Okita, Ito, Sonoda, Sakurauchi, and Abe. He had watched Prime Minister Nakasone form his cabinet and plan for his visits to Seoul and Washington. All ASEAN countries had studied the Malaysian prime minister's timely and productive visit to Japan. All would welcome Nakasone's late April tour through ASEAN countries.

Ambassador Watanakun listed some of ASEAN's common goals in dealing with Japan. They wanted more joint ventures. They wanted more technology transfers. They placed the very highest priority on economic and social development programs, and for that cooperation with the United States, Western Europe, and Japan was vital, but from Japan the most was expected. None wanted any military assistance from Japan.

ASEAN countries were glad that Article 9 remained in the Japanese Constitution. Thailand was, perhaps, the least concerned over a Japanese arms build-up, and most willing to leave to Japan how much. But it was important that such forces be for defense only. Actually, Thailand now had various useful relations with Japan's military establishment. Thai cadets went to Japan's military academy. Officers attended each other's staff colleges. There were exchanges of personnel.

The history of Thai relations with Japan differed from other ASEAN countries. During World War II Thailand was allied with Japan. A Japanese army was in Thailand, but not to "occupy" it. Japan behaved respectfully. Wartime experience was different for the Philippines, Malaysia, and Singapore: memories were ugly. The Indonesian memory was more complicated: Indonesians fought against and worked with both the Japanese and the Dutch.

Memory had affected how Japan had been "discovered." There was the latecomer's surprise in the "Look East"/model-seeking pronouncements of Singapore and Malaysia. Thailand had had close and continuous links with Japan for many years longer than they.

Good relations between Washington and Tokyo were vital for Bangkok. Friction, if serious, was deeply alarming for Bangkok, and all of ASEAN.

Thailand shared with Japan some sense of its vulnerabilities. For Thailand, Vietnam and the Soviet Union were threatening. China was not so threatening to Bangkok — as it seemed to be to Malaysia and Indonesia. Bangkok viewed China optimistically, even over the longer term, with the future slightly clouded only by evidence of Sino-Soviet detente and some anxiety about what would happen to China after Deng. Those possibilities also seemed to worry Tokyo.

GENERAL SAYIDIMAN SURYOHADIPROJO, INDONESIAN AMBASSADOR
(February 1, 1983)

General Sayidiman Suryohadiprojo was Indonesia's ambassador to Japan. A defense intellectual, he was close to President Soeharto, was formerly governor of the Defense and Security Institute, and was, as a cultural historian, now writing a book on Japan and the Japanese.

During the Tokugawa period, Sayidiman believed, Japan achieved forms of unity and solidarity historically unique, much more coherent than the Soviet Union or the People's Republic of China ever achieved. Japan was isolated from the world until the Meiji Restoration. As soon as it began to move into a world community, Japan's purpose was to catch up with the West, to make itself ready to deal with threats from the West, and to impose various controls on neighboring countries for that purpose. Japan was never much interested in its East Asian environment as such, except in making self-serving defensive calculations. Ten years ago Japan caught up. And now there was the beginning of a genuine Japanese concern for its total East Asian and Pacific environment. Comprehensive security reflected Japan's awareness of a need to "share," for its own self preservation. Sayidiman believed that sharing its assets with others would increase, not diminish, Japan's wealth and enhance its dignity.

The Japanese constituted a cohesive community at home, but they experienced difficulty in belonging to any group outside. In the sixth century, under Prince Shitoku, Chinese values and Buddhism permeated Japan's culture. A similarly comprehensive transformation of the Japanese mind and spirit was needed again.

Japan's neighbors accepted the desirability of a Japanese military establishment designed, exclusively, to retaliate against Soviet attack. However, they distrusted creation of a military capability that could move further afield. Instead, Japan should help other countries to improve their own defense capabilities. Japan should not patrol sea-lanes to the Middle East: it should assist the Indonesians, themselves, to carry that responsibility. Japanese assistance in Indonesia's industrialization might improve Indonesia's capability in military technology, while other forms of support in her economic development programs would enhance the nation's resilience.

Indonesians were aware of Japan's propensity for ranking countries. In Asia, China stood highest. Thailand stood high because it had never been a colony, was Buddhist (not Muslim), and had absorbed quite well its Chinese minority. Indonesia's ranking was, perhaps, among the lowest, and might be lower except for its oil and strategic location. Indonesians resented evidence of Japanese condescension and recalled Japan's exploitation/abuse of Indonesians during World War II. Notwithstanding such difficulties, the Indonesian-Japanese relationship was vital to Jakarta. In 1982–1983 Japan was Indonesia's most important trading partner, with Hongkong number two. The United States stood third.

Jakarta reacted with alarm when there was evidence of breakdown in the Tokyo-Washington relationship. Jakarta was inclined to lean towards the Tokyo position on defense disputes. It leaned towards Washington on trade liberalization issues. But, more fundamentally, it blamed leadership on both sides when disputes seemed to be getting out of hand.

Indonesia looked at the West and saw runaway individualism, materialism, and absence of collective purpose. President Reagan could have done better, but who, better, might follow him? And who would follow Thatcher? Or Kohl? Had Spengler's *Decline of the West* been a true forecast?

Included among threatening dangers in the future were, of course, China and Russia. Of these two, Indonesians were more apprehensive about China. China would not need to mount an external military threat, but only call on the support of Chinese minorities, infiltrate, and support subversive movements. The Russian navy was, of course, visible, but it was not a credible striking force; it had no capability to occupy territory, and the Russians had less potential than China for subversion in Indonesia.

Indonesians continued to trust the military capability of U.S. armed forces.

CARLOS VALDES, PHILIPPINE AMBASSADOR
(February 3, 1983)

Carlos Valdes was the ambassador of the Philippines in Japan. Chairman of a powerful "Philippine" accounting firm—the Cy Sips were "Chinese"—a lay leader of the Roman Catholic Church, he was Manila's representative at the Vatican before coming to Tokyo.

Valdes dwelt on several unconnected themes: the ease with which communist ideology/propaganda seemed to penetrate Roman Catholic societies (i.e., Latin America, Italy, the Philippines, etc.), Japan's economic potentials and opportunities in East Asia, Japan's "hidden" military powers, and the successes of the Reagan administration.

While Valdes was in Rome a Yugoslav priest had warned that communists had unusual success in subverting seminaries and convents. Filipino Catholics should be alert to that danger. Valdes agreed. But China had no such competence: its traditions and political instincts were secular. Peking's support of insurgencies in the Philippines ended after President Marcos's visit to Peking.

Japan had not properly conceptualized opportunities for itself and the region inherent in the fact that East Asia had become a market as large as Europe, perhaps larger. Investment opportunities were almost infinite, in Thailand (offshore oil), the Philippines (copper), liquid gas in Malaysia and Indonesia, and so forth. To balance accounts, Japan should open fully its market to import of agricultural produce: the ASEAN countries could feed the 130 million Japanese. Actually, Japan's market was needlessly difficult to enter. The time had come for Japan, itself, to do what it urged its trading partners to do: really liberalize trade. All would profit.

Japan would, Valdes forecast, go along with the United States on defense strategies, by increasing budget appropriations, exchanging technologies, joining the United States in straits patrols (without offending the Koreans), and so forth.

The United States was the hub of the world economy. The world had reason to be grateful to President Reagan for having restored its strength through reducing inflation and interest rates; and sustaining large, and vital, investment in advanced weapons for the United States military establishment. The greatness and power of the United States could not be denied: its failure was in transforming that reality into credible image.

NAYAN CHANDA, *FAR EASTERN ECONOMIC REVIEW* (February 2, 1983)

Nayan Chanda was the special diplomatic correspondent of the *Far Eastern Economic Review*. As a guest scholar of the University of Australia, he has been writing a book in Canberra about Southeast Asia. Now he was returning to resume his journalistic activity in Hongkong. Few analysts, over the past twenty years, matched his knowledge of Southeast Asia, and particularly of Vietnam.

Chanda had read the outline. All of its themes, questions, and implicit conclusions were in line with his own judgments on Japan. However, there was a conspicuous and serious omission: Vietnam.

How was it possible to talk about the security of East Asia without recognizing that Soviet facilities in Vietnam doubled capabilities of the Soviet fleet in the Indian Ocean? Japan shared Washington's concern over Soviet use of Danang and Cam Ranh Bay, but disagreed with Washington over what to do about it.

With hardly anybody talking about it, Japan was pursuing a largely independent strategy in Vietnam, independent from Washington's, China's, and even ASEAN's. Japan's embassies in Hanoi and Vientiane were better informed, had wider contacts, were more discreet, and were better trusted by the Vietnamese than any other. Tokyo and its representatives were guided by the conviction that Hanoi chafed under Soviet influence, wanted to be accepted by the West, and needed reassurance that China would not again attack it. Chanda offered evidence, in the form of conversations and writings of Vietnamese authorities, that Hanoi wanted it known that the Soviet Union was in Vietnam because Vietnam was threatened, and would be asked to leave if threat ended. The Soviet presence, Hanoi explained, was guarantee of Vietnam's survival, and was not otherwise wanted. Japan believed this to be so.

In largely unnoticed ways, Japan played its independent hand. Paying lip service to ASEAN, Tokyo stopped its aid to a Vietnam-dominated Kampuchea. However, while doing so, it agreed to reschedule Vietnam's debt to Japan, intervened to extend the grace period for Vietnamese repayment of debt owing to private bankers, and increased quietly Japan's media, private and official representation in Hanoi. It had continued to import seafoods, timber, and about one million tons of coal annually. Similar tactics were used in Kampuchea and Laos, always quietly and modestly, but with considerable effect. Japan wanted to show readiness to help, but without antagonizing the West or ASEAN.

The outline stated that there can be "safety in diversity": the Japanese believed this and wanted to act accordingly.

Japan's eventual interests were not just political. Vietnam's resources were diverse and substantial: tin, bauxite, manganese, iron ore, timber, coal, and offshore oil. More importantly, perhaps, was Japan's interest in a market of 55 million people, and a country where everything would have to be built from scratch one day.

Japan had tried to persuade Peking to accept the legitimacy of Hanoi's desire to live with a friendly Kampuchea and a friendly Laos. Look at the map, Chanda said: hostile forces in Laos could mortally endanger Vietnam's North-South connections.

Acutely aware of the Hanoi predicament, Japan's purpose was to ease Vietnam's anxieties, and thus make possible loosening if not ending the Hanoi-Moscow tie. For that to happen Vietnam must believe there was some certainty of finding a place in the West.

Vietnam did not fear Japan. In fact, neither did other Southeast Asian countries. Marcos might dislike some aspects of a Japanese arms build-up, but he knew he needed Japan and its good will. The Thais had no fear of Japan's military powers: on the contrary, they regarded their security problems to be "at home," and appreciated Japanese assistance in coping with them. Malaysia, Singapore, and Indonesia might dislike the notion of Japanese warships patrolling their waters, but they had no difficulty in accepting greatly increased Japanese military capability for home island defense only.

Chanda had been interested in the position taken in December 1982 by a leading Australian strategy expert who argued that Japan did not fear either the Soviet Union or China. Its two real fears were of the effect on energy availabilities of turmoil in the Middle East, and of abusive or insulting treatment of Japan by the United States and Western Europe. Australians themselves had no fear of Japan's military powers; their only anxiety was about how world recession might affect Australia's great, perhaps excessive, dependence on the Japanese market.

DEREK DAVIES,
FAR EASTERN ECONOMIC REVIEW
(February 2, 1983)

Derek Davies presided over production of a *Far Eastern Economic Review* now referred to with great respect worldwide. *Review* coverage of Japan was of high quality, especially on the business/technical side of things, but Davies' own perspective, in addition, placed Japan uniquely in a regionwide context. Few journalists could match his talent for identifying broad regional — and national — tendencies and for explaining their motivation.

Davies read and commented on the outline. He offered no complaint as to its structure and scope.

Davies believed, however, that more should be said about differences of perception *among* ASEAN countries. For Singapore and Thailand, the Soviet Union was seen to present a real threat. For Indonesia and Malaysia, China was the greater threat. The Philippines, accommodating on its soil Clark Field and Subic Bay, did not appear to be much concerned about any external threat: could absence of that sense of danger have a bearing on its comparatively poor growth performance? The highest growth countries in the region also happened to be anxious about one kind of threat or another — Korea and Taiwan, because of divided countries; Malaysia, because of communal tensions; Singapore, because it was small and lonely; Indonesia, because its government had emerged from a bloody upheaval back in 1965; and Hongkong, because its future status was unknown. Japan, of course, was acutely aware of its various vulnerabilities.

The Japanese might prefer to avoid describing the Soviet Union as an enemy. But the United States was certainly justified in using that word. Evidences of hostile intent were unmistakable in growth of Soviet naval power, creation of Soviet base facilities at Danang and Cam Ranh Bay, Soviet efforts to build up the Kampuchean Army, Soviet moves to create a naval base in Kampuchea from which to gain information about the Indian Ocean, and the far-flung, and sometimes skillful, activity of the KGB. Enemy? Davies said, on second thought, that "threatening presence" might be more accurate.

China's behavior was not comparable to Russia's. Indonesia and Malaysia were paranoiac about China, with Peking making matters worse for itself by keeping alive the distinction it drew between government-to-government and party-to-party relations. But, except for Vietnam, China was not now really threatening.

Davies could not, he said thoughtfully, accept the proposition that Japan was more discriminating in making its threat assessments than the United States. History had shown Tokyo accepting without dissenting "a tittle" from the Washington threat calculations, which led it into war with North Korea and, later, with Vietnam. Tokyo acquiesced, however, without accepting any moral responsibility for collaboration, even under circumstances when Washington was warning other friends that they must choose between being "with us or against us." Instead, Japan learned how to be disassociated, and still make a great deal of money. Only ex post facto did Tokyo develop a strategic rationalization for "having its cake and eating it," confronting an enemy and not calling it one.

The outline had usefully laid out elements in Japan's comprehensive security concept. There were, however, omissions and possibly misleading implications suggested. For example, Japan showed no great realism in making itself ready to take military action. There was not enough said about the constraint of very large budget deficits on Japan's fiscal calculations. There was no hint that for Japan to be allowed to buy Alaskan oil would ease its U.S.-

Japanese trade imbalance, and would help Japan to diversify, for valid security reasons, sources of its necessary energy imports. There was not enough said about the security motivation of recent Japanese aid commitments to South Korea and to Malaysia. There was some exaggeration, perhaps, in referring to normalization of Tokyo's relations with Moscow: there was still no peace treaty.

Davies referred to his *Review's* voluminous treatment of Pacific region economic interdependencies and the way Japan's trade and investment affected crucially the growth achievments and prospects of others. Japan had been a "locomotive": the *Review* had carried data that gave numbers.[14]

The outline had referred to the region's desire for more Japanese aid. Already it was substantial. Its characteristics merited attention. Japan was a careful donor. It gave excellent technology to recipients and gave instructions on how to use it. It was discriminating in approving projects. There was little corruption in administration. The Fukuda $1 billion fund for worthy ASEAN projects had not been drawn down as much as expected because projects proposed had not survived careful analysis.

The outline had linked Japan's economic role with sustaining the legitimacy of government authority in neighboring countries. Davies agreed. It was clearly true for South Korea, for the People's Republic of China, and, to some extent, for Indonesia. For the Philippines, the presumed support of the United States was a more important underwriting of Marcos' legitimacy. But, notwithstanding their Japan dependencies, for South Korea, Taiwan, possibly Thailand, and to some extent for Indonesia, United States withdrawal from the region might be more traumatic than anything that Japan could do: to imagine effective deployment of great American power in the region had been a longstanding habit.

Davies believed that more stress should have been placed on the influence of Japan as a model. Singapore and Malaysia were openly embracing it. South Korea and Taiwan had done so more quietly. The Philippines, Indonesia, and Thailand would soon be doing so.

Japan did believe that "knowledge is power." And the outline made some correct observations. For example, "tied aid" should not be frivolously condemned: essentially it was a pragmatic, business approach to aid largely extended in the form of yen credits. Tying had had good results in facilitating transfers of cheap and efficient technologies and in bringing into East Asia what Japan had learned about appropriate technologies suitable for high-population-density societies. Hongkong was very high density, and China, with its one billion population, was only 17% cultivable: Japan knew about such environmental problems.

Japan's educational system instilled reverence for knowledge. It created an upwardly mobile path. It taught deference and respect. But there were qualifications to be made in praising the system. Knowledge became real only when sifted through Japanese eyes and ears. When individual Japanese had too much contact with foreigners they loosened their hold on other Japanese. Japanese scientists did not have a strong instinct to gain knowledge for its own sake: their interest was in applied, not pure, knowledge. Davies recalled that, three years ago, Akio Morita had observed that 60% of American and European scientists worked in their ivory towers then came up with their knowledge breakthroughs, which industry might ignore for years. Ninety-five percent of Japanese scientists, meanwhile, would have been assigned to study requirements and specifications for what was needed to exploit a particular market opportunity. When answers were provided, industry used them at once.

Davies agreed that Japan's dilemma was to invite charges of "free ride" if it did not rearm or invite expressions of alarm by neighbors if it did. Southeast Asian cries of alarm should, however, be listened to skeptically. Up until 1979 Southeast Asia largely ignored Japanese armament. In fact, after the fall of Saigon, Lee Kwan Yew was but one Southeast Asian leader who favored Japanese rearmament. In 1979 Japan joined the United States, Australia, and New Zealand in some joint exercises without drawing criticism. Deng Xiaoping visited Tokyo and encouraged Japan to build up its anti-Soviet combat capabilities.

Southeast Asian presumed alarm over Japan's present military build-up and sea-lane protection intentions was, to some extent, hypocritical. It was designed to induce Japan to put up the money for support of Southeast Asia's own military capabilities.

Davies was familiar with the concept of a Japan-financed Southeast Asian coast guard. He was unconvinced that a nonmilitary apparatus of that sort could have any relevance whatever to dealing with Soviet fleet activity. The project, for many reasons, was probably a nonstarter.

Before laying aside the outline, Davies reverted to its comment on Japan's assessment of "threat," and, in particular, to Japan's use of the term "irrational" in characterizing disturbing examples of Soviet behavior. It was, of course, absurd to regard Andropov as a liberal. However, he was an intelligent man, rational, now showing great skill in his efforts to divide the United States and its Western European allies. A time might come when he focused attention on the Washington-Tokyo relationship. He might find interesting possibilities for Russia in trends. Tokyo was deeply troubled by the condition of the American economy. It had begun to doubt the reliability of Washington's defense commitments. It suspected that Washington's China interests were historically longer and, psychically, deeper than its Japan interests. Tokyo resented being the target of unfriendly noises made in Washington. Andropov might conclude that Tokyo was ready to reconsider Japan's foreign policy orientation so as to gain greater independence and explore new frontiers, if encouraged to do so. Were Moscow to make convincingly conciliatory gestures to Tokyo with respect to the Northern Islands and invite Japan to regard Eastern Siberia as that new economic frontier, Tokyo might be tempted. Davies was not ready to forecast that even a very intelligent Andropov would make such an offer. However, Davies would not exclude the possibility. Nagano, head of Japan's Chamber of Commerce, and Doko, head of Keidanren, were to be in Moscow during February, and might have it in mind.

16
TESTS OF THE CONCEPT IN 1983

The relevance and adequacy of Japan's concept of national security, still widely viewed as being shaped by its doctrine of comprehensive national security, was tested in various ways during 1983.

The first test came with the hawkish-sounding rhetoric of an English-speaking Japanese Prime Minister during his carefully crafted, widely noticed, and highly successful visit to Washington during January. Another came with Japan's sober reaction to the shooting down of the Korean Air Lines 747 by an interceptor of the Soviet air force on September 1. Others came when President Reagan visited Tokyo in November, and Japan was obliged to take stands in the United Nations and elsewhere on events in Central America, the Caribbean, and Lebanon, and on arms negotiations. Another came with Prime Minister Nakasone's involvement in Japan's budget process for 1984.

It is important to recall that the Inoki *Report on Comprehensive National Security,* when published in 1980 at the direction of Prime Minister Ohira, was an unprecedented attempt to articulate in truly comprehensive terms the strategic concepts that should guide Japan's international behavior. The United States, Europe, and the countries of Southeast Asia had never seen anything with comparable conceptual coherence come out of Tokyo before. What gave the report its special weight and interest was that, though something new as a package, almost all of the elements in the concept had become for the Japanese media, Japanese intellectuals, Japanese politicians, and Japanese bureaucrats and diplomats well-explored terrain. What was really new was to have dared to summarize, as of 1980, the incremental evolution of the pragmatic and more or less discrete policy responses made by Tokyo from 1950 to 1980 within a constantly changing international environment.

The Inoki Report restated, in effect, what had been shown to be Japan's goals: to preserve the alliance with the United States; to help strengthen an open, competitive, nondiscriminatory world economy; to ease North-South tensions; and to create an improved "defense only" military capability. It reviewed requirements to achieve them — to maintain the stability and increase the competitive powers of the Japanese economy; to increase the amount and quality of foreign assistance — economic, cultural and technological; and to reduce vulnerability of Japan's access to food and energy. It reported on shortcomings in Japanese national performance, including the need to improve qualitatively the Japanese Self Defense Forces, within Japan's limited budget allocations.

Japanese opinion was, from the first, divided as to what the Inoki Study Group intended to recommend with respect to increasing Japan's military capability, and with respect to how Japan should assume greater national responsibility for effective functioning of a worldwide political and economic system. Some viewed the report as presenting a rationale for substantial arms build-up, some as an elaborate rationale for not doing so.

Actually, the Inoki Report was to become a comprehensive working agenda for ongoing review of Japan's tactical options within broadly settled policy guidelines. It did little more than to invite marginal changes in assigning priorities for use of national resources for meeting medium- and long-term requirements to sustain Japan's competitive powers in an uncertain, unpredictable, and sometimes hostile world environment.

THE BUDGET

Japan's annual budget process has been, in the most clear and authoritative way, Japan's application of its comprehensive national security concept to government decision making. Japan's perceived vulnerabilities have been economic, political, and military. Speeches, pronouncements, and communiqués have been rhetorical gloss, but every year the budget numbers have revealed Japan's calculation of real national security requirements, at home and in Japan's foreign relations. Observers of Japanese politics look in vain for evidence of judgmental "ideological" compulsions in the vocabularies of prime ministers like Miki, Ohira, or even, recently, Nakasone. A prime minister's intimate involvement in a prolonged and exacting budget process has called upon him to make common-sense calculation of what, at home and abroad, a truly comprehensive strategy for national survival required. None has been able to escape the harsh logic of the numbers produced by the Ministry of Finance. Ironically, Nakasone did not ask for a greater increase in the 1984 defense appropriations than had been requested by Ohira in 1980, or by Suzuki in 1981 and 1982.

THREATS: REGIONAL AND GLOBAL

Tokyo has tried to separate politics from economics for 30 years and still tries to do so. Thus Japan assesses military danger within a frame made up of nearby neighbors, whose capabilities and supposed intentions regionally are subjected to scrupulous analysis, but without noticeable overattention to presumed ideological compulsions of Moscow, Pyongyang, Hanoi, and Peking.

The American frame for assessing military threat, in contrast, is global and is deeply influenced by Washington's proclaimed ideological presuppositions with respect to Soviet intention in every troubled corner of the world. Perhaps perversely, Japan seems often to fear Russian adventurism nearby less than do Americans from a distance.

MUTUAL DISTRUST

Though their threat analyses differ, both Washington and Tokyo regard their alliance as the linchpin for security in the Pacific region. Linchpin status notwithstanding, late 1982 was a time when they confronted each other angrily over many economic and defense issues. Fred Bergsten, formerly assistant secretary of the treasury, offered an explanation why: such anger happens, historically, when the value of the dollar is too strong—largely because of Washington's fiscal and financial responses to structural vulnerabilities in the American economy. Though Japan could not be fairly held responsible for Washington's management of fiscal and financial policy (e.g., budget deficits, high interest rates, tax cuts, etc.) Japan was widely blamed nevertheless for their consequences (e.g., for loss of American competitive strength and for unemployment) (see Appendix IV). In late 1982 mutual distrust and recrimination between Washington and Tokyo became dangerously intense.

On the Japanese side, there was doubt that Washington could deal with U.S.-Japanese economic questions without resort to vengeful protectionism. Many suspected racism in an American tendency to condemn the Japanese more harshly than Europeans when the behavior of both was more or less indistinguishable. Japanese saw in the Reagan administration's unrestrained readiness to invest in military strength a principal cause of likely large U.S. budget deficits over years to come, high interest rates, strong dollars, loss of competitiveness of American products in both domestic and foreign markets, and a malignant spread of demands for trade protectionism. They bridled at U.S. efforts to align friendly countries in a moral crusade against the Soviet Union. They were horrified that American military authorities could talk about protracted nuclear war-making. Listening to Washington's talk about strategic priorities in Western Europe and in the Middle East, Japanese even harbored some doubt about the reliability of U.S. commitments to stand up to the Russians in East Asia.

Meanwhile, Washington's distrust of Japan was fed by dissatisfaction over Japan's runaway bilateral trade imbalance, over Japanese competition in the area of high technology, over the supportive intention of Japan's so-called target industry policy at home, over conviction that the Japanese market was unfairly closed to American exports, and over the (unfounded) conviction that Japan had manipulated the weak exchange rate of the yen so as to promote its exports. Heated emotion, particularly in the Congress and in labor circles, was stirred by the fact that Japan was spending less than 1% of its GNP for defense, thus inviting the charge that Japan was getting a competitively lucrative free ride on the backs of the American taxpayer. Distrust spread further, to scorn for Tokyo's soft and wishful assessment of the Soviet military threat, to mistrust of Japan's sincerity in claiming readiness to bear any kind of fair share of the burden of maintaining world security, and even to skepticism that Japan would ever take the steps needed to give the matrix of its military establishment any real combat capability.

1983: A YEAR OF REAPPRAISAL

Seen in a historic context, that distressing confrontation had its silver lining. Japanese and Americans learned to talk about it openly, still as friends. When Nakasone and Reagan met, in Washington, at Williamsburg, and in Tokyo, the mere exchange of frank opinions did wonders in clearing the air — even prompting some speculation that a new and daring entente between Tokyo and Washington might be in the making. At the so-called Shimoda Conference, held outside of Washington in September 1983, dialogue between Americans and Japanese was refreshingly open, forthright, and amiable. There seemed to be prospect for the kind of constructive in-depth consultation strongly recommended in a joint conference report released last winter by the United Nations Association of the United States and the Asia Pacific Association of Japan.

This favorable shift of tendency can be fully appreciated only if we recall that shortly after Prime Minister Nakasone's January conversations with President Reagan in Washington, senior officials in Tokyo had forecast the early demise of the concept of comprehensive national security. They had forgotten, perhaps, that when, as head of the Defense Agency in 1970, Nakasone published Japan's first defense white paper, his view on weapons matched that of the 1980 Inoki Report. Also they had forgotten that Nakasone had addressed a symposium at Tokyo University in 1978 in which what he had to say about "comprehensive security" anticipated even in wording the Inoki Report.[15]

Continuities in attitude towards "comprehensive security" were demonstrated when in August 1983 Prime Minister Nakasone convened an eleven-member study council — created not long before — to consider questions related to peace. Nakasone directed this council to reassess Japan's concept of comprehensive national security. It had, it seemed, become a political necessity for him to tell the Japanese voter that he embraced much the same comprehensive strategic doctrines as his predecessors.[16]

THE WAR-FIGHTING TABOO

However, there is one important subject that is almost never discussed at all, even privately amongst Japanese: war-fighting by Japanese forces. I made this discovery in Tokyo during January 1983 when I found that it was not possible to discuss in depth with anyone a plausible scenario for actual war-fighting by Japan's armed forces anywhere. Even Japanese who strongly favored significant increases in Japanese defense spending were unable to discuss how a nonnuclear Japan could, as a practical matter, fight a limited conventional war. Japan could not alone even "skirmish" in Japanese waters or Japanese airspace with a Soviet adversary and be sure to keep the encounter contained. Imagined combat scenarios involving Japanese and Soviet forces (e.g., standing up to nuclear capable Soviet Backfires) always took for granted that Soviet strategic capabilities could never be deterred by Japanese conventional forces alone: only in combination with U.S. strategic capabilities could Japan rationally engage the Russians. And if a truly effective American deterrent, including its nuclear elements, was known to be present and ready to fight, a large Japanese combat capability might, actually, be redundant.

During the tense hours and days following the Soviet shooting down of Korean Air Lines flight 007, Japan showed that it had a significant unnoticed capability to deter, without flaunting war-fighting capability. Japanese monitoring facilities gathered information that made possible precise reconstruction of the event. What Japan revealed formed the basis for challenging Moscow to account for the behavior of its pilots and established a factual frame for a postmortem on the somewhat mystifying behavior of Washington, Seoul, and even Tokyo itself during critical hours preceding "termination" of the flight. Had all concerned — but above all Moscow and its military commands — known that Tokyo constantly monitored such proceedings step by step, the tragic event of September 1 might never have occurred.

And Japan has only begun to understand and exploit the deterrent potentials of military "knowledge." It has only begun to call upon its scientific, industrial, and technological communities to flesh out what I think of as the "AWACS concept" of deterrence for Northeast Asia: creation for coordinated defense services of an elaborately comprehensive high-technology capability — radar, electronic, acoustic, photographic, cryptographic — to gather and swiftly retrieve all information bearing on threats to the peace. For Japan to undertake and enlarge this probably high-cost mission would forestall surprises, would be a meaningful form of burden sharing, would become a critical factor in influencing Japan's own and Washington's readiness to accept informed combat involvement in crisis situations, would underlie Japan's own decisions as to the precise mix of "limited" war-fighting equipment Japan itself needed, and could be justified to Japanese taxpayers as a military mission without inherent aggressive capability.

In light of the aftermath of the Nakasone-Reagan conversations and the 007 shooting down, a main agenda item for Americans and Japanese talking through common security interests should be to reconcile Japan's unwillingness itself, and alone, to contemplate military combat with Washington's proclaimed readiness to fight, if necessary, strategic wars for global purpose. Such a consultation—with participation by labor and representatives from Congress and the Diet—should determine, if possible, how both allies can profit from forms of burden sharing that would not require either side to abandon its concepts of strategic necessity, regional and global, or even to try to "coordinate" those differing concepts.

For any such accommodation to be achieved would require that Japan, in addition to reconsidering how to spend its $11–13 billion defense appropriations, make global commitment of all of its nonmilitary instruments for forestalling economic and social turmoil and war prevention. This should be done with something like the imagination on something like the scale of what the United States undertook to do after World War II. Conscious that Washington and the Third World look to Tokyo for such leadership, Japan has already set forth the possible uses of a multibillion-dollar global infrastructure development fund to which it would be a disproportionately large contributor (see Appendix V). And more recently, Japanese participants agreed to a Trilateral Commission recommendation that Japan contribute $3 billion to IDA resources.

On the American side, it would require Washington to understand that Japan will find no great comfort merely in witnessing growth of a huge American strategic war-fighting capability to deter the Soviet Union: the United States should also invest its best intellectual skills and institutional capabilities in pursuit of worldwide arms control/disarmament arrangements. In that connection, Japan would try to be supportive.

A rereading of the Inoki *Report on Comprehensive National Security* shows that Japan is prepared, conceptually, to collaborate with the United States in such a joint effort. Washington should not cause Japan to reverse or to revise its declared strategic purposes. Japan's legitimately global interests and powers should not be subordinated to Washington's qualitatively different global intentions. Rather, Washington should encourage Tokyo to flesh out its own basic concept of real comprehensive security, to pay the costs of its own knowledge- and region-oriented military establishment, and to take the lead in imaginative use of nonmilitary instruments to preserve the peace globally.

APPENDIX I.
NATURAL RESOURCES —
OVERSEAS DEPENDENCY AND
WORLD TRADE SHARE
BY SELECTED COUNTRY (1981)

	Degree of Overseas Dependency[a] (%)					Share in World Trade[c] (%)				
	Japan	U.S.A.	Germany, F.R.	France	U.K.	Japan	U.S.A.	Germany, F.R.	France	U.K.
Energy[b]	84.8[c]	15.3[a]	56.6[a]	80.9[a]	4.0[a]	13.4[a]	19.0[a]	7.6[a]	7.1[a]	3.4[a]
Coal	83.4[c]	-13.0[a]	-3.6[a]	60.5[a]	2.6[a]	26.3[a]	0.7[a]	3.8[a]	12.1[a]	2.0[a]
Oil	99.8[c]	36.7[a]	95.4[a]	98.8[a]	7.0[a]	14.1[a]	18.8[a]	6.4[a]	7.3[a]	3.5[a]
Natural Gas	90.9[c]	4.6[a]	69.8[a]	72.3[a]	24.0[a]	10.4[a]	19.2[a]	20.5[a]	9.5[a]	4.9[a]
Iron Ore	99.6	29.2	96.5	99.6	88.9	41.1[a]	10.9[a]	16.6[a]	5.5[a]	3.3[a]
Copper	95.9	24.3	99.8	100.0	99.8	23.4[a]	11.3[a]	13.4[a]	8.8[a]	7.2[a]
Lead	87.7	59.7	91.3	90.9	99.1	6.6[a]	5.8[a]	13.4[a]	5.6[a]	26.2[a]
Zinc	65.4	58.8	70.3	86.3	94.1	9.0[a]	18.2[a]	12.9[a]	10.5[a]	7.3[a]
Tin	98.4	100.0	100.0	100.0	64.2	21.2[a]	31.7[a]	12.2[a]	7.5[a]	4.5[a]
Aluminum	100.0	64.1	100.0	-239.2	100.0	20.0[a]	15.9[a]	14.8[a]	8.4[a]	4.0[a]
Nickel	100.0	91.6	100.0	100.0	100.0	5.6[a]	37.9[a]	13.9[a]	8.7[a]	6.7[a]
Wood and Lumber	68.3[a]	1.0[a]	22.4[a]	14.8[a]	68.8[a]	21.9[a]	17.8[a]	6.7[a]	4.5[a]	7.3[a]

a) Rate of foreign dependence is calculated as follows $\dfrac{\text{Import Volume} - \text{Export Volume}}{\text{Domestic Production Volume} + \text{Import Volume} - \text{Export Volume}} \times 100$

However copper, lead, zinc, tin, aluminum and nickel are calculated as follows $\left(1 - \dfrac{\text{Domestic Mineral Output}}{\text{Consumption of Metal}}\right) \times 100$

b) In oil equivalent terms for coal, coke, oil, natural gas, hydro and nuclear generated electricity c) FY 1981 d) 1980 e) For copper, zinc and aluminum, the share of ores, ingots and alloys (unprocessed) for lead in and nickel, the share of ingots and alloys (unprocessed). For iron ore lead, zinc, tin, aluminum and nickel, figures used were in value terms, data for other natural resources were in physical terms. Source MITI. *White Paper on International Trade. 1982, 1983.*

Reprinted by Permission, from Toshio Matsuoka, Ed., *Japan 1983: An International Comparison* (Japan: Keizai Koho Center, 1983), p. 60.

REAL GNP GROWTH	INFLATION	UNEMPLOYMENT
% Average	Consumer Prices	% Labor Force
Annual Increase	% Increase	

APPENDIX II.
DOMESTIC ECONOMIC PERFORMANCE

	CAPITAL FORMATION			R&D EXPENDITURE			INDUSTRIAL PRODUCTION % Annual Growth		
	% Average Annual Increase constant prices		As % GDP	% Average Annual Increase constant prices		As % GNP	% Annual Average	%	
	1970-73	1973-80	1979	1963-73	1973-79	1979	1967-73	1973-80	1981
U.S.A.	6.5	-0.4	18.1	1.3ᵃ	2.0	2.4	4.0	2.0	-8.0
Canada	8.9	2.9	22.5	5.9	2.3	0.9	6.2	1.8	-3.0
Japan	9.4	1.8	32.0	13.0	5.9	2.0	11.9	3.2	5.0
EEC	4.0	0.8	20.9	n.a.	n.a.	n.a.	4.7ᶠ	1.8ᵍ	n.a.
France	6.8	1.1	21.3	6.8	3.4	1.8	6.8	1.7	4.0
W. Germany	3.3	1.5	22.7	3.0ᵇ	3.9	2.3	7.5	1.2	0.5
Italy	1.7	1.0	18.9	8.2	1.8	0.8	5.1	3.3	0.5
United Kingdom	2.9	-0.3	17.8	1.5ᶜ	2.9ᵈ	2.2ᵉ	3.1	0.0	-1.0

a) 1964-73.   b) 1969-73.   c) 1964-72.   d 1972-78.   e) 1978.   f) 1970-73.   g) 1973-79.

Sources: CAPITAL FORMATION: OECD, *National Accounts* (Vol. 1, 1951-1980), fourth coming; Eurostat *Review, 1970-79.*
R&D EXPENDITURE: OECD "Gross National Expenditures on R&D 1963-79" (1982).
INDUSTRIAL PRODUCTION: UN *Statistical Yearbook* and *Monthly Bulletin, Statistics* (various years); 1981 figures from *The Economist* (27 February 1982).

Reprinted by Permission, from Nobuhiko Ushiba, Thierry de Montrial, and Graham Allison, "Sharing International Responsibilities Among the Trilateral Countries," Unpublished Report, March 1982, Appendix, p. 13.

	REAL GNP GROWTH			INFLATION Consumer Prices			UNEMPLOYMENT % Labor Force		
	% Average Annual Increase		% Increase	% Average Annual Growth		% Increase	Average	Average	End of Yr.
	1960-73	1974-80	1981ᵃ	1961-73	1973-80	1981ᶜ	1960-73	1973-80	1981ᶜ
U.S.A.	4.2	2.4	1.9	3.6	9.3	9.0	4.9	6.8	8.4
Canada	5.4	2.6	3.0	3.9	9.4	11.5	5.3	7.7	8.2
Japan	10.5	4.2	2.9	6.1	9.9	3.0	1.3	2.0	1.2
EEC	4.7	2.2	n.a.	5.0	10.9ᵇ	n.a.	n.a.	4.6	6.2
France	5.7	2.9	-0.5	4.7	11.1	13.0	2.1	4.8	8.8
W. Germany	4.8	2.3	-0.6	3.6	4.8	6.5	0.8	3.3	6.5
Italy	5.2	2.8	-0.9	4.7	17.1	18.0	3.4	3.5	9.1
United Kingdom	3.2	0.9	-3.4	5.7	16.0	12.0	2.9	5.1	11.4

a) Based on preliminary IMF data.   b) 1973-79.   c) 1981 data from *The Economist* (27 February 1982).

Source: REAL GNP GROWTH: IMF, *International Financial Statistics*; Eurostat, *Review, 1970-79*.
INFLATION: *UN Statistical Yearbook, Monthly Bulletin of Statistics*; Eurostat, *Review, 1970-79*.
UNEMPLOYMENT: Eurostat, *Review, 1970-79, UN Statistical Yearbook* (various years).

APPENDIX III.
RELATIVE POSITIONS OF
GROSS NATIONAL PRODUCTS
OF SELECTED COUNTRIES (1951-1982).

	Japan		USA		Germany, F.R.		France		U.K.	
	Amount (US $ billion)	Index (U.S.A. =100)	Amount (US $ billion)	Index (U.S.A. =100)	Amount (US $ billion)	Index (U.S.A. =100)	Amount (US $ billion)	Index (U.S.A. =100)	Amount (US $ billion)	Index (U.S.A. =100)
1951	14.2	4.3	328.4	100.0	28.5	8.7	35.1	10.7	41.4	12.6
1955	22.7	5.7	398.0	100.0	43.0	10.8	49.2	12.4	53.9	13.5
1960	39.1	7.8	503.8	100.0	70.7	14.0	60.0	11.9	71.9	14.3
1965	88.8	12.9	688.1	100.0	115.1	16.7	99.2	14.4	100.2	14.6
1970	203.1	20.5	992.7	100.0	184.6	18.6	145.5	14.7	124.0	12.5
1975	498.2	32.2	1,549.2	100.0	418.2	27.0	339.7	21.9	234.5	15.1
1978	963.3	44.5	2,163.8	100.0	642.2	29.7	476.6	22.0	318.6	14.7
1979	998.9	41.3	2,417.8	100.0	761.3	31.5	576.6	23.8	412.2	17.0
1980	1,040.1	39.5	2,633.1	100.0	816.5	31.0	657.1	25.0	525.5	20.0
1981	1,139.3	38.8	2,937.7	100.0	682.8	23.2	572.6	19.5	504.3	17.2
1982	1,060.0	34.6	3,059.3	100.0	659.4	21.6	–	–	473.8	15.5

Note: Current U.S. dollar figures are calculated according to the annual average exchange rates of the IMF, *International Financial Statistics* U.S.A. = 100 for all years.

Source: Bank of Japan, *Comparative International Statistics*, 1966, 1977, 1983.

Reprinted by Permission, from Toshio Matsuoka, Ed., *Japan 1983: An International Comparison* (Japan: Keizai Koho Center, 1983), p. 4.

APPENDIX IV.
"THE DOLLAR, THE YEN AND
U.S. TRADE" (EXTRACTS)*

THE DOLLAR PROBLEM

The substantial overvaluation of the dollar in the exchange markets, in terms of the underlying competitive relationship between the United States and the other major trading countries, is by far the most critical trade problem now faced by the United States.

. . . The deterioration of the trade balance was far greater than the decline in the housing or automobile industries, and has been the single most important cause of the current recession.

Moreover, throughout the postwar period, dollar overvaluation has been the single most important "leading indicator" of an outbreak of protectionist trade pressures in the United States:

- In the late 1960s and early 1970s, import controls were imposed for the first time on steel and extended substantially on textiles and apparel; the House actually passed the highly restrictive "Mills bill"; and Congress seriously contemplated the Burke-Hartke proposals, which would have blocked most U.S. imports of goods and most exports of capital and technology. Yet unemployment was relatively low during much of this period.

- In the mid-1970s, barriers were raised on shoes and color television sets; restored for steel; and intensified once again for textiles and apparel. All this occurred while the United States was in fact recovering from the recession of 1975.

- During the past two years, barriers have been imposed or extended in four major industries (autos, steel, sugar, textiles/apparel) despite the clear ad-

*Reprinted by permission, from C. Fred Bergsten, "The Dollar, the Yen, and U.S. Trade," House Committee on Ways and Means, *Current Exchange Rate Relationship of the U.S. Dollar and the Japanese Yen,* 97th Congress, 2nd Session, 1982.

herence of the administration to market approaches, including free trade. This time, of course, the impact of dollar overvaluation is intensified by the record postwar level of unemployment.

THE YEN DIMENSION

The overvaluation of the dollar is most critical vis-à-vis the Japanese yen for both quantitative and qualitative reasons.

Quantitatively, the dollar-yen misalignment is more severe than the misalignment between the dollar and any other major currency. From late 1978 until early November 1982, the dollar had risen by over 50 percent in value against the yen. During that period, U.S. inflation exceeded Japanese inflation (on most indices) by over 20 percentage points. Thus U.S. international price competitiveness had deteriorated against Japan by over 70 percent in four years. Is it any wonder that the U.S.-Japan trade imbalance has already soared to record levels and that a major crisis exists in economic relations between the two countries?

The qualitative impact of the dollar-yen imbalance is much greater than the impact of the dollar-DM or other imbalances because of the intensity of U.S. trade competition with Japan—both within the United States and Japanese markets, and in third markets around the world. This competition is far greater than between the United States and Germany, or any other country whose currency is also severely undervalued. A primary manifestation of this U.S.-Japan trade intensity is of course the spate of protectionist trade proposals aimed at Japan which have come (or will come) before this Subcommittee, notably the "local content" legislation for the automobile industry and the "reciprocity" bill earlier this year.

During the present period, however, there is no evidence that Japan has been manipulating a weaker yen.

Indirectly, however, two Japanese policies have contributed significantly to creating such a high degree of yen undervaluation. First, Japanese interest rates are very low by international standards. Coupled with the very high interest rates which have prevailed in the United States over the past two years, partly due to the loose fiscal policy of the current administration and the resultant reliance on monetary policy to fight inflation, the result has been a sizable incentive to shift funds from yen into dollars.

All of these factors have undoubtedly contributed to the undervaluation of the yen. However, I believe that the very powerful effects of a second Japanese policy—the liberalization of its capital markets from late 1980—may be even more important.

Thus, the structural change in Japan's policy toward its capital account must have been a major factor in the subsequent weakness of the yen. This change was urged on Japan by the United States and other countries, and is surely the correct long-term policy. Japan is the second largest market economy in the world; its currency and capital markets can and should be major participants in international financial activities just as it participates so actively in trade and other economic endeavors. It can even be argued that, over time, internationalization of the Japanese capital market would make it far more difficult for Japan to maintain interest rates well below international levels — and hence preserve an undervalued yen.

. . . The pace of net capital outflow from Japan has simply overwhelmed its current account surpluses and pushed the yen to levels which are far too low to sustain in terms of trade relationships between Japan and other countries (including, but by no means limited to, the United States). Hence any immediate effort to restore proper strength to the yen will almost certainly have to interrupt, at least temporarily, the liberalization of the Japanese capital market.

. . . We are in a race against time: protectionist trade pressures seem likely to overwhelm our political process in 1983 or 1984 absent clear, substantial and continuing correction of the currency misalignment which promises within a finite period to restore some modicum of equilibrium in economic relationships between the two countries.

It would thus seem prudent to adopt some or all of the following measures as soon as possible, *inter alia* to restore proper exchange rate relationships among the dollar, yen and other key currencies:

• *further substantial reductions in U.S. interest rates*

• *aggressive foreign borrowing by the government of Japan and its Parastatal Entities*

• *temporary limitations on capital outflows by Japanese institutional investors*

• once the trend has clearly turned, *joint intervention in the exchange market by the U.S. and Japanese* (and perhaps European) *monetary authorities*

• *encouragement of private "bandwagon" movements which would complete the needed realignment*

The cardinal issue remains the need to understand that the overvaluation of the dollar, particularly vis-à-vis the yen, is the central trade issue now facing the United States. Its impact on trade and on the U.S. economy is enormous, and its impact on trade policy could be devastating.

APPENDIX V.
"A GLOBAL 'NEW DEAL'"*

Stashed in Yashuhiro Nàkasone's briefcase at Williamsburg (main story) was a plan to build a world community of nations fortified with reasonable expectations for a fairer distribution of the planet's created wealth. Already dubbed a "global New Deal," it calls for the rich countries to spend $500b., over 25 years, on Third World development. This plan is the brainchild of neither Nakasone nor the Japanese government but of the Mitsubishi Research Institute, a huge, commercially funded "think-tank" headed by Masaki Nakajima, who proposed the gigantic spending plan and has tirelessly promoted it.

Among the suggestions outlined in the briefing carried by Nakasone:

- An expressway from Manchuria to Western Europe

- A tunnel under the Strait of Gibraltar

- A sea-level canal through the Isthmus of Panama and another cutting southern Thailand

- A dam across the Bering Sea between Siberia and Alaska, diverting arctic currents and moderating the climate of the North Pacific

- A channel to let the Mediterranean Sea flow into an immense dry basin below sea-level in Egypt, changing weather by inducing rain

- An artificial lake in the middle of Africa to irrigate an area of arid, wretched Sahel larger than Germany and England put together

- An aqueduct-tunnel carrying the waters of the Brahmaputra under the Himalaya; and

- Turbines in the ocean to turn the flow of currents into electricity.

The plan is known officially as the Global Infrastructure Fund (GIF). Its magnitude, sweep and daring would stun economists accustomed to the nar-

---

*Reprinted with permission, from "A Global 'New Deal,'" *Asiaweek,* June 10, 1983, pp. 28-29.

row confines of conventional budgeting — where most world leaders live. But the prime minister of Japan has called it "thrilling." In the Diet a few weeks ago he declared his belief that it will become "fundamentally necessary" simply because "people on the same planet share a common destiny." Said Nakasone: "The 'global New Deal' or a similar concept should be put up for discussion at a summit."

Other leaders have shown support for the plan. Among them: Indira Gandhi, who invited Nakajima to Delhi last year so she could be personally briefed; Sheikh Ahmad Zaki Yamani, the Saudi oil minister, who feels his own country's aid funds could have achieved more; World Bank president William Clausen, who expressed qualified admiration for the idea in a meeting with Nakajima in Washington three weeks ago; and, in Japan, former prime ministers Takeo Fukuda and Zenko Suzuki. Significantly, too, the plan is ardently supported by Toshiwo Doko, who as chief of Japan's Keidanren, or Federation of Economic Organisations, is titular head of the nation's business world.

The scope of the plan is so vast that its leading proponents worry that it will be seen as mere futurology. Among them is Dr. Norio Yamamoto, a senior researcher who accompanied Nakajima on a pre-Williamsburg mission to gather U.S. support for the GIF. In Tokyo last week he worried aloud that publicity over some of the grander, more mind-boggling proposals may divert attention from the basic concept — that is, revitalising the world economy by pumping funds into Third World countries on a scale not envisaged since the Marshall Plan at the end of World War II.

"These projects are only examples of what might be done, not specific proposals," frets Yamamoto. "It's the investment of the $500 billion that counts. How it's spent would be a matter for international consultation."

The name Mitsubishi on the proposal's title-page should give pause to conventional economic planners whose tendency may be to scoff at boldness and imagination. Considered collectively, it is the mightiest corporate machine in the world. Largest, most cohesive of the six giant enterprise groups which raised Japan from the rubble of defeat to the pinnacle of economic success, the Mitsubishi group of 28 companies (and, now, some 3,000 subsidiaries and affiliates) was instrumental in Japan's "economic miracle."

That hackneyed term could acquire a breathtaking new relevance if applied globally, but at Williamsburg the opportunity didn't arise. The participants at the conference table were more concerned with their own problems, and those problems were hardly irrelevant to the Nakajima Plan. President Ronald Reagan's fiscal policies center on less government spending, not more, Britain's Margaret Thatcher is similarly bent on curbing government's role while France's François Mitterrand, though basically a spender, is economically beleaguered at home and in no position to think of much else. Apart from Nakasone, the only rich-nation leader who seems openly receptive to the plan is West Germany's Helmut Kohl.

What are the objections to the GIF concept? Politicians of the North say the proposed fund is too large and can't be raised. Some monetarists say it would be inflationary. Socialists in North and South say the money would simply flow back as profits to big business. Conservationists worry that some of the more spectacular projects would endanger the natural environment. A few leaders of the South suspect it's just another scheme to fleece them. And pessimists of all shades have labelled the whole thing impossibly utopian.

That the plan has a surrealistic flavour isn't denied by Mistsubishi Research Institute. Nakajima himself has called the schemes "engineers' dreams." But as a former general manager of Mitsubishi Bank, much of his working life has been devoted to turning dreams into working reality. Less than 30 years ago, when Nakajima was a key decision maker at the bank, the notion that Japan might overtake the U.S. in automobile production — or that Mitsubishi Motors might one day produce more cars than the United Kingdom — was also a dream.

Contemporary self-interests aside, Nakajima's scheme is eminently feasible. In essence, the GIF would be a gift from the North to the South, to the tune of $13b. a year. With the multiplier effect of the investment, the cumulative amount would reach $500b. within 20 years. Japan, the U.S. and West Germany would be the largest (and equal) contributors, but oil-rich, capital-surplus countries — though much less in evidence today than in the recent past — would also contribute. The recipient countries of the South would be billed for nothing except what is locally available (labour, for example) and, in general, wouldn't be required to pay investments back.

Why should the rich countries give so much? Nakajima's respnse is the most convincing of all answers: self-interest. All of the schemes envisaged in the plan are highly capital-and technology-intensive, he explains, and the machinery that they'll require can be purchased only in the North. Investment on the scale imagined would expand output in the North, promote industrial growth and reduce unemployment. At the same time, it would lift the lives of millions in the South, creating jobs, boosting productivity and increasing the flow of national funds for education and health. The present overcapacity of industrial plan could be taken up, and a state of industrial health such as has not been known since the first oil crisis would slowly take shape. Meanwhile, sounder economies in the South would create demand for more industrial equipment from the North.

Maybe so, say the critics — but wouldn't it set off an endless nightmare of global inflation? No, says Mitsubishi Research Institute. The think-tank's analysts point out that though $500b. could be easily the greatest sum ever pledged to development, it would still be less than global spending on arms and military equipment. If just 2%-3% of military spending were diverted to the GIF, there would be no adverse effect on the economies of the North. Quite the reverse; tanks and submarines, while great stimulators of economies when contracts are awarded, are not themselves productive — unlike irrigated fields and power generators.

Where would the fund be headquartered? "Singapore, Hongkong — somewhere in the newly industrialised parts of the world," suggests Yamamoto. "Certainly not in New York or Paris." Or, for that matter, Tokyo. Yamamoto and his associates are conscious that some doubters inevitably will see the GIF as another sure winner for Japanese business. He counters by asserting that the Americans, and for that matter the Russians, have much more experience in huge engineering projects than Japan.

Visionary Nakajima, meanwhile, insists that perspective is the key to understanding his global New Deal. The world, he feels, should learn to differentiate between "international," implying one nation's dealings with others, and "global" thinking that would seek benefits for all the earth.

NOTES

1. Article 9 of the Japanese Constitution states: "Aspiring sincerely to an international peace based on justice and order, the Japanese people forever renounce war as a sovereign right of the nation and the threat or use of force as means of settling international disputes.

   In order to accomplish the aim of the preceding paragraph, land, sea, and air forces, as well as other war potential, will never be maintained. The right of belligerency of the state will not be recognized."

2. "Asian Economic Survey," *Asian Wall Street Journal,* (October 4-8, 1982); and Derek Davies et al., "Community begins at home," *Far Eastern Economic Review* (December 10, 1982) pp. 67-72.

3. *Development Cooperation: 1981 Review* (Paris: Development Assistance Committee of the Organization for Economic Cooperation and Development, 1981) pp. 174-175; and *The Military Balance 1981-1982* (London: International Institute for Strategic Studies, 1981) pp. 112-113.

4. The Comprehensive National Security Study Group, "Strengthening Defense Capability," *Report on Comprehensive National Security* (July 2, 1980) pp. 41-47.

5. The Air Force Office of Public Affairs describes AWACS as follows (courtesy of Major General James C. Pfautz): "The E-3A Sentry aircraft is an airborne warning and control system (AWACS). It provides all-weather surveillance, command, control and communications needed by commanders of U.S. and NATO tactical and air defense forces.

   The radar and computer systems on the E-3A can gather and present broad and detailed battlefield information. Data are collected as events occur. This includes position and tracking information on enemy aircraft and ships and location and status of friendly aircraft, naval vessels and ground troops.

   In its tactical role, the E-3A can provide information needed for interdiction, reconnaissance, airlift and close air support for friendly ground forces, as well as information for commanders of air operations to gain and maintain control of the air battle.

   As an air defense system, the Sentry can detect, identify and track airborne enemy forces far from the boundaries of the U.S. and NATO countries. It can direct fighter interceptor aircraft to these enemy targets."

6. Robert W. Barnett, "ASEAN'S unguarded coasts," *Foreign Policy* No. 38 (Spring 1980): 117-125.

7. Donald Wise, Ed., *Asia 1983 Yearbook, Far Eastern Economic Review* (1983): 8-9.

8. Ibid., except for the data on Laos, which are from the *Asia 1982 Yearbook,* pp. 10-11.

9. S. David Freeman, "Nuclear power isn't scary — These reactors are," *Washington Post* (November 28, 1982) section C, p. 1.

10. Ross Terrill, *Mao* (New York: Harper & Row, 1980), p. 287.

11. Economic Cooperation Bureau, "Japan's Economic Cooperation," Japanese Ministry of Foreign Affairs (July 1, 1982) p. 18.

12. Ibid., p. 19.

13. The Comprehensive National Security Study Group, "Summary of the Report," *Report on Comprehensive National Security* (July 2, 1980) p. 8.

14. Derek Davies et al., "Community begins at home," *Far Eastern Economic Review* (December 10, 1982): 70.

15. Yasuhiro Nakasone, "Toward comprehensive security," *Japan Echo* 5(4) (1983): 32-39.

16. In late spring of 1984 *Tokyo Shimbun* reported on the work of the Council. The Council's initial examination of economic and financial elements in Japan's national security had been completed. And now, according to *Tokyo Shimbun,* Prime Minister Nakasone had directed the Council to complete by November reexamination of needed defense expenditures, but in a context of national security requirements also with respect to energy, rare metals, food, and official development assistance resources for other countries. It was expected that the Council would find that "comprehensive national security" costs would come to at least 2% of GNP. However, it was suggested that the Council would have the opportunity to recommend that in the budget process 3% replace 2% as a goal for security spending, with a stipulation that something between 1.2% and 1.5% be the goal for defense spending alone. *Tokyo Shimbun* foresaw that the tradition of a 1% ceiling for defense spending would be exceeded, but in the context of concurrent increases in appropriations for non-military resources devoted to comprehensive security. The work of the Council was not, of course, completed, but, according to *Tokyo Shimbun,* Prime Minister Nakasone was hoping to enlarge both military and non-military appropriations for Japan's security by dignifying the concept of comprehensive national security through the processes of budget presentations.

ACRONYMS

AAM	Air-to-Air Missile
ABM	Antiballistic Missile
AEW	Advanced Early Warning
ANZUS	Australia, New Zealand, and the United States (defense pact)
ASEAN	Association of Southeast Asian Nations
ASM	Air-to-Surface Missile
ASW	Antisubmarine Warfare
AWACS	Airborne Warning and Control System
BADGE	Basic Air Defense Ground Environment
CCC and I	Communications-Command-Control and Intelligence
CINCPAC	Commander in Chief Pacific Forces (U.S.)
DAC	Development Assistance Committee
ELINT	Electronic Surveillance
EMP	Electromagnetic Pulse
EURATOM	European Atomic Energy Commission
FY	Fiscal Year
GDP	Gross Domestic Product
GNP	Gross National Product
IAEA	International Atomic Energy Agency
IBM	International Business Machines Corporation (U.S.)
IMF	International Monetary Fund
INF	Intermediate Nuclear Force
IISS	International Institute for Strategic Studies
JCS	Joint Chiefs of Staff (U.S.)
JDA	Japan Defense Agency
JDP	Japanese Democratic Party
JSO	Japanese Staff Office
KGB	Committee for State Security (Soviet Union)
LDC	Less Developed Countries
LDP	Liberal Democratic Party (Japan)
MITI	Ministry of International Trade and Industry (Japan)
NAM	National Association of Manufacturers (U.S.)
NSC	National Security Council (U.S.)
NATO	North Atlantic Treaty Organization
ODA	Official Development Assistance
OECD	Organization for Economic Cooperation and Development
OTH	Over-the-Horizon Radar
R and D	Research and Development
SAIS	School for Advanced International Studies of Johns Hopkins University
SAM	Surface-to-Air Missile

UAE	United Arab Emirates
USAF	United States Air Force
WEIS	World Economic Information Service

INDEX

ABOUT THE AUTHOR

Robert W. Barnett, now a Resident Associate of the Carnegie Endowment for International Peace in Washington, D.C., was born in Shanghai, China. He received his college education from the University of North Carolina, where he was elected to Phi Beta Kappa, and was named a Rhodes Scholar at Oxford University. He was a Rockefeller Fellow in New York, and a Fellow at Yale and Harvard Universities. After military service with the Fighting Tigers in China during World War II, he joined the United States Department of State where he eventually served as the Deputy Assistant Secretary of State for East Asian and Pacific Affairs from 1963 to 1970. From 1970 to 1979, Mr. Barnett was Vice President of the Asia Society, and Director of its Washington Center. Mr. Barnett has written several books and reports on Pacific issues and dozens of articles for newspapers such as the *New York Times*, the *Washington Post*, *Baltimore Sun*, and *Mainichi Shimbun*, and for journals including *Foreign Policy, Foreign Affairs*, and *Far Eastern Economic Review*.